Investigating the biggest Questions in Christianity

Karsten Wille

Greatness University Publishers
www.greatnessuniversity.co.uk

ISBN: 978-1-913164-31-7
ISBN-13: 978-1-913164-31-7

DEDICATION

This book is dedicated to my nephews Giles and Kurt. *'Do your best to present yourself to God as one approved, a worker who does not need to be ashamed and who correctly handles the word of truth'.* 2 Timothy 2:15

CONTENTS

ACKNOWLEDGMENTS

I would like to thank my family for giving me the time to write this book. A special thank you to my mother for the editing.

PREFACE

This book aims to analyse scripture in the context of all Bible evidence relating to the most frequently asked questions in Christianity. These top ten topics have divided many in the body of Christ confirmed in various different teachings of the church. Many of the answers to these questions in scripture are clear cut, whereas others need a lot more scrutiny by weighing up all scripture and not just particular chosen verses to come to an informed decision. My intention is not to push for a particular teaching of the church, but rather ask the most important question; what does the text say?

Approaching the answers to a lot of these topics will be the Christian who makes an important distinction between what belonged to the law in the Old Testament and what adheres to grace in the New Testament. My intention is to delve into scripture, commenting on the customs and cultures of the times they were written and the audiences they were meant to capture. Scripture is only useful if we rightly divide the word of truth, which is consequently only possible if we study ourselves approved (2 Timothy 2:15). This can only be done by digging heavily into scripture and gaining an idea of ancient customs, Judaic culture and the laws commanded by God at that time. This will also be enhanced in some topics by researching what the Old Testament Hebrew and New Testament Greek has to say in regard to certain key words which will naturally throw a lot more light on a given topic.

Context is crucial when dealing with God's word and no quote says it better than by Dr. Ben Witherington: "A Text without

a context is just a pretext for what we want it to mean..."
(Witherington 2009 p 41) Some of the ten most frequently
asked questions in Christianity are philosophical, whereas
other questions will be on an ethical and moral basis. When
investigating many of the answers to these questions it will be
vital to take it from a scriptural standpoint that the word of
God does not change. Jesus (the word) is the same yesterday,
today and forever (Hebrews 13.8) and our Father does not
change like shifting shadows (James 1:17). God's word is
unchanging and eternal. He revealed to Malachi 'I am the
Lord and change not' (Mal 3:6). This also means that he has
not changed his mind according to the moral guidance he has
given us. Many progressive Christians including those who
would disagree with a lot of the moral fabric of scripture
would argue that the Bible is outdated and needs to be
brought in line with modern day thinking. This is why I will
be avoiding 'special revelation', as evidence. Any answers to
the questions will not rely on subjective evidence based on the
way society feels about a given situation that changes its mind
over time, but will be based on the unchanging objective word
of God. In the same way I will not be engaging in 'identify
politics', to come to any informed conclusion. The stance this
book will take, is that all scripture is God breathed: *All
scripture is given by inspiration of God, and is profitable for
doctrine, for reproof, for correction, for instruction in
righteousness'.* 2 Timothy 3:16

WHERE DID CAIN GET HIS WIFE?

This can be a frequently asked question when I teach topics on creation or covenant. This is also a major question which has caused many to doubt a literal creation and is cited as one of the main evidences against it. At first it seems to be a difficult question, but it may not be as problematic as one would first imagine. Surprisingly, the topic stumps most Christians. The reason why it emerges so much in general knowledge questions is to address validity in scripture and this may be because the Bible is not clear on specifically who Cain's wife was. We have no indication how old Cain was when he killed his brother Abel.

(*Cain and Abel*, 16th-century painting by Titian)

Cain was the first person to be born and Abel was the first person listed in the Bible to die. Abel's death occurs when Cain is jealous due to the fact that God accepted Abel's sacrifice and not his. So, we see the first murder and death appear in the Bible.

"And Cain talked with Abel his brother: and it came to pass, when they were in the field, that Cain rose up against Abel his brother, and slew him." ... And it came about when they were in the field, that Cain rose up against Abel his brother and killed him." Genesis 4:8, KJV

Both Cain and Abel were farmers. Cane grew produce and Abel worked with livestock. This would also clearly indicate that they were adults due to the nature of their work and skill. We know that Adam and Eve also had many more sons and daughters who were not specifically named in the Bible (Genesis 5:4). The only children who are named specifically as children of Adam and Eve were Cain, Abel and Seth. Being that Cain and Abel were adults we do not have specific clarity as to whether they already had existing families. Now of course alarm bells may be going off in your head in regard to incest and Biblical teaching on the subject, but we need to remember that it was only outlawed by God later on in scripture. Even Abraham approaching two thousand years later was married to his half-sister:

'Abraham replied, "I said to myself, 'There is surely no fear of God in this place, and they will kill me because of my wife.' ^{12} *Besides, she really is my sister, the daughter of my father though not of my mother; and she became my wife.* ^{13} *And when God had me wander from my father's household, I said to her, 'This is how you can show your love to me: Everywhere we go, say of me, "He is my brother."'''* Genesis 20:11-13

It is only after the giving of the law to Moses in the book of

Leviticus that we see incest as we would understand it today outlawed in scripture.

'The nakedness of your father's wife you shall not uncover; it is your father's nakedness. [9] The nakedness of your sister, the daughter of your father, or the daughter of your mother, whether born at home or elsewhere, their nakedness you shall not uncover. [10] The nakedness of your son's daughter or your daughter's daughter, their nakedness you shall not uncover; for theirs is your own nakedness. [11] The nakedness of your father's wife's daughter, begotten by your father — she is your sister — you shall not uncover her nakedness. [12] You shall not uncover the nakedness of your father's sister; she is near of kin to your father. [13] You shall not uncover the nakedness of your mother's sister, for she is near of kin to your mother. [14] You shall not uncover the nakedness of your father's brother. You shall not approach his wife; she is your aunt. [15] You shall not uncover the nakedness of your daughter-in-law—she is your son's wife—you shall not uncover her nakedness. [16] You shall not uncover the nakedness of your brother's wife; it is your brother's nakedness. [17] You shall not uncover the nakedness of a woman and her daughter, nor shall you take her son's daughter or her daughter's daughter, to uncover her nakedness. They are near of kin to her. It is wickedness. [18] Nor shall you take a woman as a rival to her sister, to uncover her nakedness while the other is alive'. Leviticus 18:8-18

It is clear that since Adam and Eve were the first human beings on earth, it would be their offspring that would also be fruitful and multiply. It is also evident that Eve was made from Adam as she was bone from his bone and flesh from his flesh (Genesis 2:22-23). Intermarriage as shown in the book of Leviticus was only outlawed by God when it was seen that it was no longer necessary for procreation and God knew that the gene pool had changed. The reason why it is so dangerous for incest to take place today is due to the likelihood of genetic abnormalities occurring. Recessive characteristics in similar genetics can become dominant, posing a risk to offspring. These recessive characteristics become far less likely when people come together with each other from different gene pools as both parents are unlikely to have these same recessive traits. We need to remember that Adam and Eve were created perfect and did not have any abnormalities. All genetic information in humanity today was present in Adam and Eve. Procreation with family members without defects and a clean gene pool would not have been dangerous. However, nowadays the human genetic code over a period of time will have met problems, where any genetic abnormalities will have been amplified and passed down the family tree.

The misconception concerning Cain leaving the presence of the Lord and taking a wife in the land of Nod to the east of Eden is a Bible translation issue. If we look at the scripture clearly, it indicates that they had a child together called Enoch.

[16] Then Cain went out from the presence of the LORD and dwelt in the land of [a] Nod on the east of Eden. [17] And Cain knew his wife, and she conceived and bore Enoch. And he built a city, and called the name of the city after the name of his son—Enoch. Genesis 4:16-17

This does not imply that he went there to get married and find a wife or take a wife, as all it indicates is that the King James 'to know', means sexual relations. Even the NIV version uses the words 'make love'. The offspring from Cain and his wife was Enoch. From this offspring came a city after the son of this name. God gave Adam and Eve two commandments in the garden and that was to not eat from the tree of the knowledge of good and evil and to be fruitful and multiply, fill the earth and subdue it. Since Adam was already 800 years old when Seth was born (one of the very few named children), one can imagine how many offspring they had in that time period.

"And the days of Adam after he had begotten Seth were eight hundred years: and he begat sons and daughters:" Genesis 5:4

The next question that naturally emerges is of course the ages people reached in those days, but this seems to have been the norm for that time period, until God himself puts an age cap on humanity in Genesis. In this next chapter God drastically reduces their life expectancy.

' And the LORD said, ͤ"My Spirit shall not ͩstrive ᶦwith man forever, ͤfor he is indeed flesh; yet his days shall be one hundred and twenty years." Genesis 6:3

Reaching a very old age in the book of Genesis is an amazement to many including Pharaoh when he meets Joseph's father Jacob (Israel) for the first time. Jacob informs him that his ripe old age was nothing compared with his forefathers.

⁹And Jacob said to Pharaoh, "The days of the years of my ᵃpilgrimage are one hundred and thirty years; few and evil have been the days of the years of my life, and they have not attained to the days of the years of the life of my fathers in the days of their pilgrimage." Genesis 47:9

When viewing the account of Cain, it is clear that he was very frightened leaving his home, not because of wild animals, but because of other people. He was concerned about living life as a beggar and feared for his very life. This indicates that Adam and Eve had clearly had far more offspring who in the meantime would have broken off and started tribes of families elsewhere.

"Behold, thou hast driven me out this day from the face of the earth; and from thy face shall I be hid; and I shall be a fugitive and a vagabond in the earth; and it shall come to pass,

that every one that findeth me shall slay me." Genesis 4:14
KJV

When looking at the Biblical accounts of Adam and Eve, you have an approximation of 1500 years until the account of Noah's ark, providing plenty of time for pro-creation, separation and different civilization (or lack of it for that matter). After Noah the whole of humanity is once more reduced to a single family with their spouses to start afresh. The origin of man is a very popular study, so much so that I wrote another entire book on this, taking from scripture and scientific evidence to conclude that science itself confirms that we all come from two original ancestors, with no actual evidence of ape-like appearance (Creation: On the Origin of Man). Many struggle with the concept of the first human beings as a literal Adam and Eve. In contrast, believing in energy accidentally colliding with the primordial soup, bringing about life in the form of conscious observers is likely to require far more faith.

References and Wider Reading

Dr. Georgia Purdom, Creation Basics, Answers Magazine July 1, 2014

Karsten Wille, Creation: On the Origin of Man, Greatness University Publishers, 2020

WHAT DOES THE BIBLE SAY ABOUT PASTORS BEING WOMEN?

I think the best way of dealing with this topic is to look at how women fulfil roles in ministry as a whole. If we think long and honestly about this question, it is unlikely that the Body of Christ would be where it is today without the service of women and the caring and nurturing nature they bring to the church in physical service and especially in prayer. If you give a woman a word she will give you a sentence. If you give her a sentence she will give you a paragraph. You give her a paragraph she will give you a book. If you give her a house, she will give you a home (Munroe 2001). It is this talent and touch of a woman that can bring about lasting change or even multiplying what she has been given, especially in the area of organization and wisdom. She forms the caring bond in the domestic church. All Godly marriages can testify to that. Most men feel lost without their wives. As we have heard many a time, that 'behind every great man there is a great woman' (The Port Arthur News Feb 1946). Possibly in many cases even a greater woman. It is not unusual to come across women in ministry who are indeed more talented than their husbands in eloquence of speech and presentation. This is why it is important to view the husband and wife as a unit. The better the husband turns out, frequently the more admiration goes to the supportive and loving wife who got him to the place he is. It is the recognition of this family unit which is so important, which goes beyond the titles.

If we generalize female church attendance compared with male, it usually becomes quite clear that congregations on average consist usually of 60% of women and 40% of men.

Very often women are very eager to be involved and fulfil more roles in ministry compared with their fellow brothers in Christ. It is clear that women have always played a major role in not just the running of the church but also the growth of it. Women were largely the ones witnessing the crucifixion of Christ when most of the disciples through fear had absconded.

⁵⁵'And many women who followed Jesus from Galilee, ministering to Him, were there looking on from afar'. Matthew 27:55

²⁵'Now there stood by the cross of Jesus His mother, and His mother's sister, Mary the wife of Clopas, and Mary Magdalene'. John 19:25

Not only were they present at his crucifixion, but Jesus chose to reveal himself first to women after his resurrection: an unusual move for the time as a woman's testimony in court was not counted as reliable. The apostle Paul placed much emphasis on the ministry of women as he frequently greeted many of them by name in his letters. Many of these women are described not just as co-workers, but also clearly people who served and contributed to the benefit of the Body of Christ in the churches they were residing in:

⁶'Greet Mary, who labored much for us'. Romans 16:6

¹²'Greet Tryphena and Tryphosa, who have laboured in the Lord. Greet the beloved Persis, who labored much in the Lord'. Romans 16:12

²'I implore Euodia and I implore Syntyche to be of the same mind in the Lord. ³⁽ᵃ⁾And I urge you also, true companion, help these women who laboured with me in the gospel, with Clement also, and the rest of my fellow workers, whose names are in the Book of Life'. Philippians 4:2-3

10

'To [s]the beloved Apphia, Archippus our fellow soldier, and to the church in your house' Philemon 1:2

'And I urge you also, true companion, help these women who laboured with me in the gospel, with Clement also, and the rest of my fellow workers, whose names are in the Book of Life'. Philippians 4:3

This whole topic, however, does bring division to the church for most Bible-believing Christians, especially concerning the interpretation of scripture that either forbid to allow women to speak in church or even have authority over a man. This especially comes to the forefront when viewing scriptures like 1 Corinthians 14:34 and 1 Timothy 2:12-14:

[34]'Let [s]your women keep silent in the churches, for they are not permitted to speak; but they are to be submissive, as the law also says'. 1 Corinthians 14:34

[12]'And I do not permit a woman to teach or to have authority over a man, but to be in silence. [13]For Adam was formed first, then Eve. [14]And Adam was not deceived, but the woman being deceived, fell into transgression'. 1 Timothy 2:12-14

The needs of the Body of Christ were many and offices at the time were created in order to meet that need. Nowadays if we view church offices they certainly do vary from church to church. Many modern churches hold the position of elder and deacon as the same. However, it is important to note that they were not actually the same office. The office of the deacons was at first created to serve in a physical capacity to meet the ever increasing needs of the church. Some theologians theorized that Pheobe was an active deaconess in the church of Cenchrea. The reliability of this notion, however, really depends on which Bible translation you are using. Here is a quote from the New King James:

'I commend to you Phoebe our sister, who is a servant of the

11

church in Cenchrea', Romans 16:1

The translation of the word 'diakonos', does indeed seem to mean deacon. An issue, however, arises if one assumes that the position of a deacon today is the same as it was then. Some translations use deacon, others use servant. In the first century it is theorized that a deacon was responsible for the care of the sick and the poor, not mixed in with the responsibilities of an elder, pastor or bishop. Ministry to the poor mainly consisted of widows, orphans and the sick. She was viewed as a person of wealth who was able to contribute to the upkeep of people who were in need, thus regarded as a person of great influence.

Another favourite verse attracting much attention concerning the role of Apostles is Romans 16:7 concerning Andronicus(male) and Junia (female?). This has been largely put forward by Linda Belleville:["Ιουνιαν ... επισημοι εν τοις αποστολοις [tr.:"Junia...notable among the apostles"]: A Re-examination of Romans 16.7 in Light of Primary Source Materials", New Testament Studies, 51, pp 231-249.] The NIV reads:

'Greet Andronicus and Junia, my fellow Jews who have been in prison with me. They are outstanding among[¹] the apostles, and they were in Christ before I was'. Romans 16:7 (NIV)

The footnotes in the NIV accompany the words 'esteemed by', in relation to 'outstanding among'. This once again plays into the hands of which translation of the Bible you choose to use. The New King James version reads:

⁷'Greet Andronicus and Junia, my countrymen and my fellow prisoners, who are of note among the apostles, who also were in Christ before me'. Romans 16:7 (NKJ)

The ESV uses the words *'they are well known to the Apostles'*. This translates very differently from: 'outstanding among the Apostles'. Then there is the further contention in the Greek as to whether Junia is actually female. The New King James and King James uses the word countrymen. Whether Junia is male or female, general understanding of all translations available to this verse is that they were Paul's compatriots who were in Christ before he was. These two people appear nowhere else in scripture, which casts doubt on the likelihood of them being apostles. Keeping in mind what the Apostle Paul writes in Timothy and Titus, it is highly unlikely there were female Apostles. This then becomes one of these situations whereby you could liken it to a lawyer looking at a book of law and attempting to find a legal loophole. One would need to question if this one verse is sufficient to re-write history books or for that matter accepted church doctrine.

The issue of disagreement is not just these verses, but in relation to the culture then and of modern day society. Were these verses only meant for the era in which they were written? After all, since the emancipation gathering speed over a period of now 100 years, society has changed immensely. With this in mind many people believe and interpreted Galatians 3:28 in a way that frees them to fulfil roles traditionally held by men in the Church.

²⁸'There is neither Jew nor Greek, there is neither slave nor free, there is neither male nor female; for you are all one in Christ Jesus'. Galatians 3:28

Others may maintain that 1 Timothy 2:12-14 is still applicable in the modern era since the foundation of this scripture is not a cultural issue, but rather a moral issue rooted in the divine order of creation. On a cultural level, it is often cited that the only reason women did not have leadership roles in the church specifically attributed in scripture, was due to the fact that the Bible was written at a time when women were not considered worthy to be educated. One may question this slant when viewing who Jesus picked to be his disciples. Most of them were uneducated fishermen. One of them was qualified as a tax collector, but considering scholarly qualifications, we may have Paul, but he was a later convert, a considerable time after the ascension of Jesus. The early Church consisted of those whom society had not held in high esteem.

Before speaking of the eligibility of who should be a priest or pastor, it may be worth investigating at the very least who qualified as an elder. 1st Peter 5:1-4 gives us the answer when describing Shepherds overseeing the flock:

'*5 The elders who are among you I exhort, I who am a fellow elder and a witness of the sufferings of Christ, and also a partaker of the glory that will be revealed: ² Shepherd the flock of God which is among you, serving as overseers, not by compulsion but [b] willingly, not for dishonest gain but eagerly; ³ nor as being [b] lords over those entrusted to you, but being examples to the flock; ⁴ and when the Chief Shepherd appears, you will receive the crown of glory that does not fade away'.* 1 Peter 5:1-4

The qualifications put forward by Peter for an elder is characterized by a specific Greek word that is used in the New Testament 66 times, translating as 'seasoned male overseer'. This Greek word is '*presbuteros*'. In the English language we do not delve much into the masculine, feminine and neuter nature of nouns, because we don't generally have them attached to the word 'the'. 'Presbuteros' is a masculine word. The feminine form of this word is 'presbutera'. This feminine word is never used in scripture in conjunction with elders or shepherds. If we view the uniformity of the following scriptures, we can see what determines the qualifications of either an overseer or pastor or even bishop.

'This is a faithful saying: If a man desires the position of

a [b.]bishop, he desires a good work. [2]A bishop then must be blameless, the husband of one wife, temperate, sober-minded, of good behaviour, hospitable, able to teach; [3]not [b.]given to wine, not violent, [b.]not greedy for money, but gentle, not quarrelsome, not [b.]covetous; [4]one who rules his own house well, having his children in submission with all reverence [5](for if a man does not know how to rule his own house, how will he take care of the church of God?); [6]not a [b.]novice, lest being puffed up with pride he fall into the same condemnation as the devil. [7]Moreover he must have a good testimony among those who are outside, lest he fall into reproach and the snare of the devil'. 1 Timothy 3:1-7

[6']if a man is blameless, the husband of one wife, having faithful children not accused of [b.]dissipation or insubordination. [7]For a [b.]bishop must be blameless, as a steward of God, not self-willed, not quick-tempered, not given to wine, not violent, not greedy for money, [8]but hospitable, a lover of what is good, sober-minded, just, holy, self-controlled, [9]holding fast the faithful word as he has been taught, that he may be able, by sound doctrine, both to exhort and convict those who contradict'. Titus 1:6-9

The qualifications of an elder, pastor or even bishop seem to be very clear from the above passages including the scriptures mentioned earlier in 1 Timothy 2:12, as a woman has not been given authority to teach or to be able to exercise authority over a man. These duties involve leading a congregation, whilst overseeing the spiritual growth of the people of God and evidently according to scripture are exclusively reserved for men. Although many would like to invoke **Galatians** 3:28 to prove that there is 'neither man nor woman' in the body of Christ, it is important to note that this verse does not reflect the culture or climate of today in a political sense. Galatians was concerning the moving away from the religious laws of the Jews and 3:28 as a direct result of the Gospel was concerning baptism and salvation and being one in Christ, not a turnaround of the roles of men and women. It was a statement in regard to our equal value in the eyes of God. The whole issue can frequently be interpreted as men versus women scenario, but it is important to realize that there are many women who believe women should not serve in the capacity of elder, pastor or bishop and equally many men who believe they should. It is important also to realize that this is not an issue of inequality, but rather an issue of whether the Bible is being interpreted correctly. Just because God has given us different roles, does not mean we have less value.

To add to the discussion already made concerning Phoebe as a deaconess, Priscilla is frequently brought into the limelight in Acts 18. Both Aquila the husband and Priscilla the wife, were known as faithful ministers of Christ. The ranking of importance and emphasis usually rests on Priscilla as she is named first in scripture with Aquila as more of a subsidiary. It is very true that both Priscilla and her husband taught the Gospel to Apollos in their home more adequately, who only knew the baptism of John (Acts 18:26). Of course, nowhere is it recorded that Priscilla after sharing in this counselling session at home with her husband, pastored a church or had a platform ministry leading a congregation. There is no evidence that she stood against the guidelines of 1 Timothy 2:11-14, in anything she did.

Biblical evidence which is often cited in favour of women serving in the capacity of a pastor are found in the Old Testament when viewing female leadership by Miriam, Deborah and Huldah. It is true that these women had special ministries and were known for their faith and quality of leadership. However, one would question why Old Testament accounts of women who held positions of leadership become relevant to the issue of pastoring a church, performing duties as an elder or bishop. The New Testament is a new covenant for God's people with a structure of leadership that is exclusively set out for the Body of Christ, not in relation to the Hebrew nation or any other Old Testament characters. It is also these figures of Miriam, Deborah and Huldah who formed more the exception to the rule than what is presented in the whole of the Old Testament. Even the Temple in Jerusalem had a special place called the court of women, which was the outer forecourt of the Temple where women were permitted to enter. The teachings on this subject of Orthodox Jews will vary considerably from their progressive reform Jew counterparts, who choose to interpret Old Testament law in light of the modern day, putting commandments up for interpretation rather than necessarily following them to the letter.

(Picture credit: Deborah beneath the Palm tree c 1896-1902: James Tissot)

In conclusion and scripturally speaking, the involvement of women is clearly seen in the Bible, but cannot be supported in the role of elder, pastor or bishop. Beyond the titles no doubt there will have been women of integrity who in remote areas or times of crisis will have held the fort. Equally, some of the biggest ministries to date have been led by women for women and further accomplishments in a tremendous humanitarian capacity. Any limitations concluded does not mean a woman cannot pray or prophesy from the platform or serve as a worship leader, youth minister, children's director or specifically run women's ministries from the platform without which the Body of Christ would not be able to function effectively. The specific restrictions set upon women are adopting spiritual authority over male adults. As a reasoned consequence, any position or role in the church that does not depend on bestowing spiritual authority over a man is therefore permissible. Women are therefore clearly able to perform most roles in the church. There are many female pastors in the world today including priests in some liturgical denominations, but they will only cite evidence in support of their ministry by relying on subjective morality (changing with the times) or will support their choice of vocation dependent on their own 'special revelation'. If we are asking what the text says, scripture itself does not support it.

References and Wider Reading

The Port Arthur News Feb 1946

Linda Belleville, A Re-examination of Romans 16.7 in Light of Primary Source Materials", New Testament Studies, 51, pp 231–249.

Two Views on Women in Ministry, Revised, Edited By: Stanley N. Gundry, James R. Beck By: James R. Beck, ed. More in Counterpoints: Bible and Theology Series ZONDERVAN, 2005

Dr Myles Munroe, UNDERSTANDING THE PURPOSE AND POWER OF MEN a book for men and the women who love them Whitaker House 1030 Hunt Valley Circle New Kensington, 2001

WHAT DOES THE BIBLE SAY ABOUT TITHING?

This is going to be one of the longest chapters in the book, as I have devoted an entire book already to this question 'Tithing: Reviewing Scripture in Context'. When researching what the most frequently asked questions in Christianity were, it came as no surprise that it came up.

To be able to answer this question effectively, I will firstly have to define what the tithe actually is. Most churches neglect to define the practice according to what the Bible says it is, compared with how we have understood it as part of church cultural giving in the past. I have chosen to use older text books for the definition as the meaning of the word 'tithe' using online Bible dictionaries has lined up more with church culture over time, rather than the actual definition the Bible gives us. Hodder and Stoughton illustrated Bible Dictionary defines the tithe as the following:

The practice of giving a tenth of one's income or property as an offering to God. The custom of paying a tithe was an ancient practice found among many nations of the ancient world.

The practice of giving a tenth of income or property extends into Hebrew history before the time of the Mosaic Law. The first recorded instance of tithing in the Bible occurs in Genesis 14:17-20. After returning from rescuing Lot and defeating his enemies, Abraham met Melchizedek, 'the King of Salem' and 'priest of God most high'. The text states simply that Abraham gave Melchizedek a tithe of all the goods he had obtained in battle. The author of the book of Hebrews, in recounting this episode, considered the Levitical priests who descended from Abraham and who appeared centuries later as having paid tithes to Melchizedek through Abraham (Heb. 7:1-10). There is no recorded demand for a tenth. Neither an explanation given about why Abraham gave a tithe to Melchizedek. Jacob also, long before the law of Moses, promised that he would give to the Lord a tenth of all he received (Gen 28:22). The Law of Moses prescribed tithing in some detail. Leviticus 27:30-32 stated that the tithe of the land would include the seed of the land and the fruit of the tree.

In the New Testament the words tithe and tithing appear only eight times (Matt 23:23; Luke 11:42; 18;12; Heb. 7:5-6,8-9) All these passages refer to Old Testament usage and to Jewish practice. Nowhere does the New Testament expressly command Christians to tithe. However, as believers we are to be generous in sharing our material possessions with the poor and for the support of Christian ministry. Christ himself is our model in giving. Giving is to be voluntary, willing, cheerful, and given in the light of our accountability to God. Giving should be systematic and by no means limited to a tithe of our incomes. We recognize that all we have is from God. We are called to be faithful stewards of all our possessions (Rom. 14:12; 1 Cor.9:3-14; 16:1-3; 2 Cor. 8-9). (Hodder and Stoughton Illustrated Bible Dictionary).

Hodder and Stoughton's definition does set the record straight as to what the tithe was. Furthermore, is very detailed concerning the appearance of the word and usage of the word in the New Testament and the requirement of giving set out in the epistles, not relating to any type of tithe by law or necessity of a given percentage.

The Zondervan Bible Dictionary also lets us know more as to what resources were tithed:

'Tithe (tenth), 10ᵗʰ part of one's income set aside for a specific use, to the government or ecclesiastics. Its origin is unknown, but it goes back far beyond the time of Moses, and it was practised in lands from Babylonia to Rome. Abraham gave tithes to Melchizedek (Gen 14:20; Heb. 7:2, 6); Jacob promised tithes to God (Gen. 28:22); Mosaic law required tithing of all produce of land and herds (Lev, 27:30-33); use for support of Levites and priests (Num. 18. 21-32); additional tithes may have been required at certain times (Deut. 12:5-18; 14:22-29); there were penalties for cheating in tithing (Lev. 27:31; Deut. 26; 13-15). Pharisees tithed even herbs Matt. 22:23; Luke 11:42). (Zondervan Bible Dictionary)

In this Bible dictionary definition, we can also see that the tithe consisted of not just a 10ᵗʰ, but in some cases and at certain times considerably more. The Mosaic Law tithe was also always paid in the form of produce of the Land or by herds of cattle, in other words 'FOOD'! I will explain more about the different types of tithes and percentages required later on, but it is important that it is understood that the 'tithe' did not consist of money, although money and currency was already in use and operation in Genesis. We only have one instance in scripture when these food items could be converted into money for the purpose of paying the tithe (Deut. 14:25-27). Furthermore, this tithe was consumed and eaten by the person tithing without ignoring the Levites who were also present. Something important to note in both Dictionary definitions is that the tithe was not simply a Jewish custom on behalf of a theocracy, but was also part of the ancient customs in all the regions of Mesopotamia and beyond which is put in a time frame in the pre-law period. Since the Bible records the word tithe in the pre-law period, with notably two important characters who are Abraham and his grandson Jacob, it may be of value to do a character study on both of them allowing you to explore the nature of the recording of the tithe.

In a study of Abraham, you will discover that most theologians agree that Melchizedek was a contemporary of the King of Sodom and was a priest who worshipped a pagan deity. He was a very great man; however, he was not a pre-incarnate Christ. In typology, however, he serves as a type of Christ: a picture of the priesthood to come, not in the order of Levi. This is not a pre-law example of the eternal moral principle of tithing. Abraham followed the ancient Mesopotamian pagan practice of tithing a tenth in the form of spoils of war. Abraham went to war to recover his family and the goods from the King of Sodom. None of the goods were his! He deliberately decided to take nothing offered to him as a reward, except for what his men had already eaten. It is common sense to realize that you cannot tithe from something that is not your own. This is pre-law and the Levitical system had not yet been established. The Patriarch acted as High priest of the family.

(Photo Credit: Rubens image)

In the case of Jacob, Abraham's grandson, the offer of the tithe to God was when Jacob was forced to abandon his father's household. We have no evidence of Isaac practising it, and Jacob's vow to God was an act of desperation when he was running for his life. The Priestly Levitical system was still in his loins through one of his 12 sons, Levi. He had no one to tithe to; furthermore, there is no evidence he made good on his promise. This is not evidence of an eternal moral principle in operation to be resurrected by the New Covenant Church. The book of Genesis did not set tithing out as a command to follow.

The command to tithe is only found in the Mosaic Law. This was the law given to Moses starting with Aaron as the Levitical High Priest; however only started in the Promised Land. Tithes were only given in food sources. Land and flock owners could only tithe from produce from the Land of Israel. Any produce outside of the Land of Israel was not considered worthy. People only tithed if they had a harvest of grain, wheat, oil and wine. Herd owners tithed from their flocks and did not have to give the best of their flocks. The best of flocks was reserved for the Priests to tithe to the Lord! The only time the tithe was not food was in (Deut. 14:25-27), if the tent of meeting for the festival tithe was too far, so the food items were sold, only to be re-bought at the destination of the tent of meeting and converted back into food. This enabled the people to celebrate with the Levites during the festival tithe once a year. The tithe was therefore eaten in the presence of the Lord! If you did not own land producing crops or herds producing cattle, then you did not qualify to tithe! People who practised any trained crafts as was typical in Jewish culture for all males of a certain age did not tithe. Metal working, carpentry, tent making, or anything of the sort did not qualify a person to tithe. Fishermen also did not tithe as fish was not on a list of items you could tithe. You could only tithe from the supernatural increase of the Land of Israel.

Non land or flock owners were entitled to give free will offerings to the temple treasury, if they so wished and during the time of the temple qualified to pay temple tax, but they did not tithe! Charitable alms could also be given.

There was not just one tithe as stipulated by all new Covenant ministers of the present day church, who vehemently try and collect them and suggest that replacement theology puts them in the present day position and authority of the Levites. This should not be a like for like theology! To collect tithe(s) plural, you had to be part of the tribe of Levi in Israel. Furthermore, not all Levites were priests. The tribe of Levi consisted of some who were priests; however, most Levites would be temple workers and would assist the priests in their duties. The upkeep of the temple required many workers on a shift system. The priests would officiate at the altar, whilst the Levites would fulfill all other duties associated with the temple from singing, to temple guarding and collection of tithes. Levites were not allowed to own land and therefore the tithe was there to sustain them through the Mosaic Law. Only the Levites could collect tithes. 10% went to the Levites who were allowed to take the food sources back to the Levitical cities for them and their families. 1% would go to the Priests who ate the tithe in the temple area. It is only the priests who had access to God in the holiest areas of the temple, anyone else would have lost their life if they would have tried. The people of Israel could only have their sin atoned through the High Priest.

18 Then the LORD said to Aaron: "You and your sons and your father's house with you shall bear the [b]iniquity related to the sanctuary, and you and your sons with you shall bear the iniquity associated with your priesthood. (Numbers 18:1)

There were specifically three tithes of food sources! Again, I need to stipulate that the word tithe in the Mosaic Law can only relate to food and there is nothing in scripture to tell us otherwise. These three tithes were:

The first tithe (Levitical tithe) The Levites were all from the tribe of Levi, some of whom were Aaronic priests. The 10% would go to the Levites and 10% of this tithe would go to the priests. The priestly tithe had to stay in the store-house and be eaten in the Temple area, whereas the rest of the tithe for the Levites could be carried off the temple site and be taken home to their families or to one of the 13 Levitical cities. Again, it could only come from the Holy Land of Israel.

[20] Then the LORD said to Aaron: "You shall have no inheritance in their land, nor shall you have any portion among them; I am your portion and your inheritance among the children of Israel.

[21] "Behold, I have given the children of Levi all the tithes in Israel as [a] an inheritance in return for the work which they perform, the work of the tabernacle of meeting. (Numbers 18:20-21)

The second tithe (Festival tithe) was the tithe that was brought directly to Jerusalem, the Holy City. The Israelites who had produce from their land, orchards, vineyards and herds would take this tithe to Jerusalem once a year and it was almost in the form of a family holiday. This tithe was in support of the festivals and a portion was consumed with the Levites in celebration with the tither's entire family. It formed a time of festivity and celebration in the presence of the Lord.

[6] There you shall take your burnt offerings, your sacrifices, your tithes, the heave offerings of your hand, your vowed offerings, your freewill offerings, and the firstborn of your herds and flocks. [7] And there you shall eat before the LORD your God, and you shall rejoice in [a] all to which you have put your hand, you and your households, in which the LORD your

God has blessed you. (Deuteronomy 12:6-7)

The third tithe (Tri annual poor tithe) was for whom the name actually suggests. It took place every 3 years. It wasn't just for the widow and the orphan, it was also for the stranger who was not originally from Israel. (Side note, strangers to Israel were not allowed to tithe) This tithe went to the place it was needed in Israel and not specifically the Holy city. We have therefore three distinctly different tithes.

[28] *"At the end of every third year you shall bring out the tithe of your produce of that year and store it up within your gates.* [29] *And the Levite, because he has no portion nor inheritance with you, and the stranger and the fatherless and the widow who are within your gates, may come and eat and be satisfied, that the LORD your God may bless you in all the work of your hand which you do. (Deuteronomy 14:28-29)*

[12] *"When you have finished laying aside all the tithe of your increase in the third year—the year of tithing—and have given it to the Levite, the stranger, the fatherless, and the widow, so that they may eat within your gates and be filled,* [13] *then you shall say before the LORD your God: 'I have removed the* [a]*holy tithe from my house, and also have given them to the Levite, the stranger, the fatherless, and the widow, according to all Your commandments which You have commanded me; I have not transgressed Your commandments, nor have I forgotten them'. (Deuteronomy 26:12-13)*

Bringing the whole tithes (plural) into the storehouse is clearly because there were three of them. Not just more than one person tithing. This also causes a discrepancy with the expectation to tithe merely 10%. The tithe consisted of 10% Levitical tithe, 10% Festival tithe and lastly the tri-annual poor tithe consisting of 3.3% every year. This was a yearly combined tithe of 23.3%. Three tithes of which 2 are 10% a year and 1 every 3 years, culminating into 23.3% of income.

Then tithing on every 7th year and 50th Jubilee year would also need to cease. So, no tithing took place on the 7th and 50th year so the land could recover and crop rotation could take place. Tithing churches today do not let you off from tithing on the 7th or 50th year!

First fruits were not a tithe! It was small enough to be collected by hand and put in a basket, or could consist of a sheaf of wheat from a field. They were to be collected by those who produced harvest and presented to the priest.

In the book of Judges, the people rejected God as their King and wanted a monarch in keeping with the pagan tribes they were surrounded with. The ruling monarch then became the person to receive the all-important 1st tithe, which cannot be described as anything less than a tax. This unpopular move was enforced by King David and Solomon. When Israel was being re-established under Persian rule, there is a good chance the King of Persia would also have benefited from this, as he was the ruling monarch. If we review the tax system in Western governments, in general it also includes the Welfare State. If you are employed, the tax which is being deducted from your salary is already used to support the poor. Your giving is not starting from zero just because you attend Church! In Germany people are leaving the Church in droves as the Church tax is unaffordable and in many cases even denying the faith!

If you are a tithe-payer being faithful to the Mosaic Law and deciding to include the tithe in the New Covenant, then you need to realize that you would only be permitted to tithe food sources from the Land of Israel. This does not include money! Food banks are becoming common place in many churches, which is a good thing! If you are deciding to agree with replacement theology, ie: equating the Levites like for like with the church starting in the book of Acts, then you may also only tithe in food. Might one suggest that turning up with non-perishable items of food every Sunday at Church will raise a number of questions!? There is also a reminder attached to this, that you cannot obey parts of the law. You would have to fulfil all the law, comprising 613 Mitzvoth. The basics of this law would include, circumcision, kosher eating and Sabbath keeping. You cannot just pick and choose which ones you want to lay to rest and which ones to resurrect!

The behaviour of the people in charge in the temple was often a source of annoyance for God, as the Priests did not always do as they were told. Eli the High priest and his sons were punished during the time of the Judges due to bad leadership (Samuel 4) leading to the glory departing. This in the Old Testament, however, was not an unusual occurrence. The Priests in the last book of the Bible, Malachi, also behaved badly in regard to lazy worship and theft. Malachi is quite a short book and easy to read, yet most people are only familiar with the verses about tithing. I will be quoting from the book of Malachi on other topics in this book in relation to God being unchanging and the issue of divorce. The structure of the book is outlined as the following:

Malachi 2:1-9; Malachi criticizes the leaders for not teaching the Law.

Malachi 2:10-16; Malachi addresses the unequal yoking of inter-marriage with other tribes, whilst divorcing their own wives.

Malachi 3:6-12; Malachi expresses God's distaste for the way the priests are trying to rob God by stealing the tithes.

Malachi 3:8-11 are chiefly the only verses most congregants are aware of concerning tithing, as it promises untold blessing if followed and the release of the devourer if disobeyed.

[8] Will a man rob God? Yet ye have robbed me. But ye say, Wherein have we robbed thee? In tithes and offerings.

⁹ Ye are cursed with a curse: for ye have robbed me, even this whole nation.

¹⁰ Bring ye all the tithes into the storehouse, that there may be meat in mine house, and prove me now herewith, saith the LORD of hosts, if I will not open you the windows of heaven, and pour you out a blessing, that there shall not be room enough to receive it.

¹¹ And I will rebuke the devourer for your sakes, and he shall not destroy the fruits of your ground; neither shall your vine cast her fruit before the time in the field, saith the LORD of hosts'. Malachi 3:8-11 (KJV)

The specific context to the most famous verses in Malachi about robbing God comes into play when we realize how the priests were behaving. The book of Nehemiah is set at the same time period as the book of Malachi and forms the basis of understanding the nature of what is going on. This is likely to be the true and actual context of the verses in relation to robbing God. The Priests who were entitled to 10% of the 10% were neglecting the Levites and robbing them of their portion. As a result, the temple had to be shut down, as the Levites decided to go to the fields to work them in order to feed themselves, neglecting their part time temple shifts. The High priest Eliashib and Tobiah the Ammonite (related to Eliashib by marriage) were certainly not living their lives in favour of Israel. Tobiah was in direct opposition to Nehemiah's restoration and rebuilding of the walls of Jerusalem and gained favour with Eliashib the High Priest, who leased the store-rooms of the Temple to him, thus allowing him to flourish bountifully in business. These store-rooms were of course for the tithes. Nehemiah gained permission from Artaxerxes of Persia to return to the newly constructed temple in Jerusalem and restore the correct order; furthermore, returning the storehouse to its proper and holy use. This required the necessary ritualized cleansing to allow this to take place, and the ejecting of Tobiah the Ammonite from the area. This is explained in Nehemiah 13:4-12. As established previously, the Church is not the people of Israel. Furthermore, the rebuke concerning robbing God was not directed to the people of Israel, but the behaviour of the Levitical Priests themselves. This has no place in a Sunday sermon requiring New Testament giving. Even if you were to reject the historical context of the book of Nehemiah, you cannot brush aside the fact that the priests were being rebuked, not the people of Israel.

Tithe-paying ministers are quick to point out that the word tithe does indeed appear in the New Testament. This, however, does not take into account when the New Covenant started. It is therefore important to realize that Jesus' entire ministry in the Gospels took place under the Old Covenant. For example, the Rich Young Ruler in Matthew 19:16 wanted to know how to inherit eternal life. Interestingly enough the whole of chapter 19 is about the law and the account of the Rich Young Ruler has more to do with keeping the Law, than giving possessions to the poor. The moral of the account holds much for us still today, but in a New Covenant context, Jesus would have emphasized the necessity of believing in Him to be granted eternal life, (Acts 16:31, 1 John 5:13) not following the rigorous law of keeping the 613 Mitzvoth to satisfy the law. Salvation under the New Covenant can't be earned, but is given as a gift (Hebrews 8:6). This free gift can only be manifest in our lives through the person of Jesus.

The Gospels, therefore, have to be contextually taken into account as under the Old Covenant. There are two instances when the word tithe is mentioned in the Gospels. The Law is yet fully operational, as all aspects of the law are still in need of being kept. The sacrificial system is in full flow and all Jewish feasts, beliefs and customs are being celebrated as prescribed in the Old Testament. John the Baptist and Jesus would have been circumcised on the 8th day, nothing according to the law would have been missed out. Now you may be wondering why I am spending a lot of time making this point about the Gospels; but this is precisely it, as anything said about tithing in the Gospels is indeed the fulfilment and requirement of the law that Jesus himself is supporting. We have two specific instances in Matthew 23:23-26 and Luke 11:41-42 that makes this evidentially clear.

[23] "Woe to you, scribes and Pharisees, hypocrites! For you pay tithe of mint and anise and cummin, and have neglected the weightier matters of the law: justice and mercy and faith. These you ought to have done, without leaving the others undone. [24] Blind guides, who strain out a gnat and swallow a camel!

[25] "Woe to you, scribes and Pharisees, hypocrites! For you cleanse the outside of the cup and dish, but inside they are full of extortion and [b]self-indulgence. [26] Blind Pharisee, first cleanse the inside of the cup and dish, that the outside of them may be clean also". Matthew 23:23-26

[41] But rather give alms of such things as ye have; and, behold, all things are clean unto you.

[42] But woe unto you, Pharisees! for ye tithe mint and rue and all manner of herbs, and pass over judgment and the love of God: these ought ye to have done, and not to leave the other undone". Luke 11:41-42

These verses will always be used by ministers who support the tithing philosophy that tithing in itself, is a New Testament/New Covenant principle, as Jesus talks about it in Matthew and Luke and is therefore applicable to us today. The theological point that needs to be grasped here, is that one must separate the idea of the literal Old Testament/ New Testament from the applied Old Covenant/ New Covenant!

The New Covenant only comes into force at Calvary and the veil being torn in two. Everything recorded before the death of Jesus in the Gospels should be regarded as literary New Testament, but Old Covenant. The next point I would like to make from both the accounts in Matthew and Luke is that there is no mention of money. The tithe in this respect for the Pharisees is something that is consumed by the body or for a better word, to flavour food in the form of mint and all manner of herbs. The weightier point I would like to make specifically regarding these verses is shown within the key word itself: 'weightier'! The weightier matters of the law, justice, mercy and faith, they had neglected. Again, we need to look carefully at the word law; furthermore, the priorities Jesus is setting as to what is more important. The Pharisees who were the priestly elite in very important positions had managed to almost exempt themselves from tithing through the Oral law that was put into writing in the Talmud (Not applicable to Christians). They merely tithed from the spices in their kitchens and gardens and in many ways behaved in a similar way as described by Malachi's rebuke of the priests in the Old Testament. Jesus was clearly not a fan of the Talmudic add-on regarding the Mitzvoth, much in the vain of the Sabbath being there for man and not man for the Sabbath (Mark 2:27-28).

If we consider any of the evidence given in the Gospels already concerning the tithe, Jesus brings up the Pharisees and specifically their hypocrisy and self-righteousness whenever the word tithe is mentioned. Tithing was, however, essential during the Old Covenant which was still in full operation up until the crucifixion, but even then, Jesus ties the topic in with those who would rather give food, than change their hearts for the better. This is no more evident than in the Parable of the Pharisee and tax collector (Luke 18:9-14). The tax collectors were the most hated people in the Jewish community as they collected funds for the Roman occupiers. People would spit on the ground or cross on the other side of the street when coming across a traitor to Israel, yet Jesus paints a very different picture when comparing a Tax Collector with a Pharisee. With the Old Covenant still applicable during this time, Jesus moves the goal posts and ups the game concerning priorities. The Old Testament law was issued so the people of Israel could respond in obedience to God's will. However, Jesus transforms the law by focusing on the attitude of the heart. In other words, he made it more perfect. Even when focusing on the Ten Commandments Jesus took things a step further. To not commit murder; people were not to be angry. To avoid adultery; people were to refrain from lust. In the like for like case of the Pharisee and the tax collector, Jesus compares two figures who traditionally according to the religious views of the day would have been at opposite ends of the spectrum, yet it is the tax collector of all people who could have been chosen who comes out justified, due to genuine repentance, rather than the Pharisee who fasts twice a week and tithes of all he possesses. The priority for Jesus is and will always be the attitude of the heart.

This also of course raises another important question. Do Jews practising Judaism still tithe today? Even in the modern day, the interpretation of the law by the Rabbis puts tithing only in the realms of the land of Israel. Farmers with produce outside the land of Israel are not obligated to tithe as a custom. The whole weight of the law is only also in effect, if there is a majority of Jews living in the land of Israel. The temple mount is missing the Jewish temple itself, and the red heifer has not been sacrificed to meet the demand of the purification rites. This means that everyone today would suffer from something called corpse contamination. This would make the tithe of no effect. Israel no longer has a Levitical system of tithing which was the very nature and purpose of the tithe. The tithe was for the upkeep of the priests and Levites. The State of Israel used to be a theocratic state that had incorporated this whole system in Government for the separation of the tithes. Please take note of the word tithes as a plural, also heavily pointed out in this chapter. Rabbis affirm that there were 3 tithes:

- First tithe *'ma'aser rishon'* (Levitical tithe)
- The second being the *'maser sheni'* (taken straight to Jerusalem)
- The third tithe *'maser ani'*, which was the tri-annual poor tithe. (Jacobs 1995)

There are some strict Jews who may donate a tenth of their income to charity called 'the money tithe', or 'wealth tax', *'maasser kesafim'*, but for the most part there is absolutely no clarity whether any form of tithe is a voluntary contribution rather than an obligation. Can I also make it clear once more, charity is not interpreted as giving to the synagogue!

There are a number of factors preventing tithing from being practised in Judaism. The issue the Jews face today is the lack of a temple standing on the temple mount. Furthermore, no ordained Levites or priests poses a very big problem for the Jews to put the law of tithing into operation. To simplify what is stated on this topic: A synagogue-attending Jew is therefore incapable of tithing and if they would try to do so, they would be violating the very law of God which would be classified as sin. How are you supposed to pay tithes without Levites? It is the absence of the temple, which puts a spanner in the works. However, should the temple be rebuilt with priests rebuilding the altars and following the sacred traditions, then every Jew with produce from the Land of Israel inside Israel would then be once more required to tithe. Worthy of noting, within those parameters only! These parameters also include the strict lineage of the tribe of Levi.

What we do know, however, as a matter of certainty, is that financial giving within the synagogue is covered by a system of buying seats within a synagogue. This clearly does not represent a ten percent tithe system and in many cases for better seats will go far beyond 10% of an annual income. This money is paid by a family where everyone has their set seat, goes straight to the synagogue and not a charitable donation (*Maasser kesafim*). The synagogue is also not to be interpreted as the Levitical priesthood or Levite. The temple mount needs to be cleansed by a red heifer: the temple was destroyed in 70AD, with not even a stone standing on top of another and there is no Levitical priesthood officiating at the altar. The Jews know that, and it was their system that was in place to begin with. Orthodox Jews are very strict followers of the 613 Mitzvah, from circumcision to kosher food-eating laws. Some Ultra-Orthodox Jews do not even mix with the gentiles, so it is clear there are many who follow the law according to every stroke of the pen. Tithing, however, cannot be followed as they lack the means to do so!

The book of Hebrews was written to attract the precise audience pertaining to its name ie: The Jews! The book was proclaiming Jesus as the New High Priest! As we have previously discussed in this chapter, there is a distinct lack of evidence regarding any mention of tithing in the New Testament or in regard to the New Covenant. The book of Hebrews, however, does mention the word a number of times. First, we need to look at the historical setting to put things in context. The book of Acts in chapters 15 and 21, talks of a struggle between Peter and Paul pertaining to the Jews and Gentiles, and the book of Galatians also throws this up with the difficulty of circumcision and those not willing to associate with the uncircumcised or non-kosher eating or Sabbath-keeping Jews. Paul really had his work cut out trying to unite the Jews who were following the law strictly and the Gentiles who at first were not considered worthy of receiving salvation. So we have two distinct groups of the faith many years after the crucifixion of Christ, some still following the Jewish festivals and going to the Temple and others whose faith alone was in Christ, whereby there would have been no justification in the law. For those still attending the Temple and all the Jewish customs, tithing may have been a procedure followed until the destruction of the temple in 70 AD by the Romans. Of course, after this catastrophic event, this would no longer have been possible. Perhaps the book of Hebrews is a further warning to make amends in keeping with Grace. Marrying this custom with the emerging church would also have raised many questions. The groups of Jews and Gentiles were to be brought under a new umbrella and that was the Church, as a body of believers in Christ.

The writer of Hebrews is addressing the book to the precise audience he is trying to convince. The Jews are still hanging on to their customs. Chapter 7 thus becomes very important as it is the only time tithing as a topic is mentioned in the New Covenant. At this point I also need to specify, that chapter 7 is not about tithing per se, but rather the importance of Jesus Christ and a better covenant. This extract is not evidence for the need of a tithe-paying church, but rather the King of Righteousness, the need for a New Priesthood, the greatness of that New High Priest and the advantages of a better covenant. It is also putting the Old Covenant to rest with all of its laws and statutes.

It can be seen that the writer of Hebrews is using the book of Numbers, specifically chapter 18 in making comparisons between the Aaronic Priesthood that was supplied and maintained by the law of tithing, with the New Priesthood in the order of Melchizedek, namely Christ. This new high Priest is eternal and completely under the spirit of Grace. This book addressed to the Hebrews presents Christ as the person who can solve their theological dilemma, in making the transition from Old Covenant to New. These better promises included better sacrifices in the form of praise and thanksgiving and of course a better system of giving under grace.

I would not normally include so much detail in a single chapter; however, as Hebrews is the only effectively New Covenant evidence of tithe being mentioned, I cannot cut corners on this one. Clarity regarding the book of Hebrews chapter 7 is essential. If we once again look at who Melchizedek was, he was a very great and respected man. He was a contemporary of the King of Sodom, therefore a pagan Gentile priest whom Abraham brought the spoils of war to in the form of a tithe, fitting with the ancient culture. Although it is stated that Melchizedek was servant of the 'Most High God', there is nothing to suggest that this reference does not refer to the Pagan deity of the time, likely to have been Baal. The God of Abraham most assuredly was not the deity worshipped by the occupants of Sodom. The King of Salem can typically be translated into the King of Peace, which is also a title appropriate for the Messiah. This does not mean that the writer of Hebrews is saying Melchizedek and Jesus are the same person or a pre-incarnate Christ: he is making a comparison in the sense of the Old Testament foreshadowing the New. As Dr Kelly writes: The writer uses Melchizedek 'typically', not 'historically'. (Kelly 2007 p 150) We therefore have a building up of this character Melchizedek to be compared to Christ the High Priest, not comparing like for like in the form of a Christophany. Just the fact that there was no record of the lineage of Melchizedek did not mean that he randomly came from nowhere, it merely meant that the records of his birth or heritage were not readily available. Jewish record keeping was immaculate and had Melchizedek made an appearance during the times after Moses, then no one would have paid tithes to him, for the very reason that you had to be from the tribe of Levi to receive tithes or officiate at the altar. Melchizedek had the limitations of mortality as did Aaron, but Christ is our High Priest forever. So we can see that the person of Melchizedek is being typified as a type of Christ as opposed to a pre-incarnate Christ. Had this person in Genesis actually been Christ, then it makes nonsense of the whole meaning of the account and God revealing himself to man through Abraham, thereby calling him out of his father's household.

The tithing references in Hebrews 7 allow the Jews to understand the person of this High Priest before the Law of Moses and then afterwards. The tithing aspect puts into perspective the authority of the individual. But there is one greater than Melchizedek and the Aaronic Priesthood, and his name is Jesus! Perfection could not be achieved through the law, but only through Christ, indicating the limitations of the Old Covenant system and tithing. Complete obedience to the law and therefore achieving Godly perfection was not possible. The entire tithing system provided for the Levitical system, but did not create a perfect person. The Priesthood therefore with all its ordinances was in need of replacing. This replacement supersedes the law, and puts the law of tithing into no effect. This moves the Aaronic priesthood under the Levitical system to a better system, which is the system that puts the believer in the position of the priest of their household. This is the domestic church. We were unable to draw near to God through the Levitical system, as that was formerly only possible for the Aaronic High Priest to do in the Temple (Heb 9:7). We can now approach God with confidence, because we are the Temple of the Holy Spirit! If the Levitical system is being undone, then so is the tithing system that sustains it. The system of Grace is beyond the law. This entire text in Hebrews 7 is not written to affirm the practice of tithing sustaining the Aaronic Priesthood, but rather the abolition of it for something better. If we read chapter 7 in its entirety, we can see how the comparison and the context unfolds. It is clear that within Christ the limiting factors are removed. There is no justification by just giving a set percentage. Nothing pertaining to the Law is suitable to sustain the Church and the five-fold ministry. The law in this context means nothing and Christ himself means everything.

Sustaining the body of Christ is not up to the natural, it is dependent on the supernatural. Jesus is therefore not limited by this old institution that has forever been laid to rest. The new covenant does not enforce circumcision, keeping of the Sabbath, Kosher eating and the like, so why is it suggested tithing is inferred in the New Testament without evidence in scripture? Melchizedek and Levi are mentioned in order to do away with the old and to make a way for the new. Had all these ordinances not been abolished including the tithe that sustained them, then we as the church would not be able to boldly approach the throne of Grace. It is the whole silence of the issue of tithing in the New Testament that lets us know that it had been laid to rest. Scripture is very specific in instructing us what to do and what not to do. Had a particular ordinance of the Old Testament been required, then the Epistles would have dealt with it. In Colossians 2:14 it is evident what Jesus did with these ordinances.

'Blotting out the handwriting of ordinances that was against us, which was contrary to us, and took it out of the way, nailing it to his cross'; Colossians 2:14 NKJ

Why some people choose to attempt to resurrect a system that was in place as if our Saviour had not finished his work is very questionable. The veil of the temple was torn in two, yet some with their actions are attempting to put it back. We cannot sew the veil of the temple back up and put God back into a box with a clear conscience.

New covenant principles of giving can only really be put into context by the person who wrote most of the New Testament epistles. The Apostle Paul! He worked more abundantly than them all (1 Corinthians 15:10). To set his credentials straight as to his authority, Paul makes the following statement to the Philippians:

'Circumcised on the eighth day, of the stock of Israel, of the

tribe of Benjamin, a Hebrew of the Hebrews; concerning the law, a Pharisee'. Philippians 3:5 NKJ

The Pharisees along with the Sadducees ran the religious show of the time. Paul, a Pharisee was so devoted to the law that he was willing at first to do anything for it, inclusive of killing Christians and looking after the cloaks of those who stoned the apostle Stephen in the book of Acts. His passion for the Old Covenant before his living revelation with Christ was going to take him to Damascus, whereby he could fulfil the mission given to him by the Sanhedrin, to wipe out the Christian population in the area or at least split up their families and send them into slavery. Here is a man who at first religiously could not have been further from Christ, yet on the road to Damascus had a life-changing experience. After his living revelation of Christ, he was never going to be the same again. He in fact gained a higher revelation of Christ than Peter (2 Corinthians 12:2-4). Without Paul, Christianity would have stayed largely with the Jews, following strict Kosher eating laws, keeping the Sabbath and circumcision as a sign of the covenant with God. Christianity would also have died out with the Jews at the time of the destruction of the temple in 70AD. If anything was a requirement in scripture he would have referred to it and made it clear for all to see, as he did not mince his words. Concerning those who were forcing the issue of the law regarding circumcision he wrote:

[12]As for those agitators, I wish they would go the whole way and emasculate themselves'! Galatians 5:12 (NIV)

If you want clarity, look no further! I don't think there are many scriptures that put things more bluntly concerning a requirement of the law being laid to rest. Now you may ask yourself why I feel the need to verify the credentials of Paul, after all his work speaks for itself. This is the precise point. Had there have been a requirement in the new covenant to tithe, let us be clear, he would have mentioned it! His blunt no-nonsense approach would have set the record straight! He would have gone into the Old Testament and foreshadowed it in the New Testament and made it a requirement and called it an eternal moral principle. Yet his silence on the issue is deafening. With all Paul endured in his sufferings, whether in persecution or lack of funds, would one not think that the person who wrote most of the New Testament would not have depended on his right to the tithe? Not once does he evoke anything relating to it in scripture or infer the need for it. He speaks of the need for support in 1 Corinthians 9:1-19. However, there is nothing pertaining to the tenth of a tenth or any relation to a percentage. Instead in 1 Corinthians 9: 1-19 we have a pattern of self-denial and the need to serve all men:

All Jewish boys were trained in a particular skill from a young age to ensure they were able to earn a living wage. Paul had the same trade as Barnabas in making tents with goat's hair and was fully self-sufficient (Acts 18:3) Assessing what Paul says in 1 Corinthians chapter 9, it is clear he was using his skill and trade to finance himself, with the occasional support from the church. He had to justify himself to the Corinthian church with Barnabas for the need of support; furthermore, feeling the need to make this request as an Apostle who had had a living revelation of Christ. It is evident that in chapter 9 he is alluding to the fact that he is being accused by the church of requesting full-time support and sustenance from them, as the apostles from the church in Jerusalem had done. He is not standing upon his rights as an apostle to receive financial support, but he does make the point, that other professions from soldiers, to grape vine farmers and herdsmen received certain benefits from their line of work. He makes it clear that he is well within his means to request right of support, yet his emphasis is not on a demand for sustenance, but rather being able to present the gospel without charge and not abusing his authority in the gospel. Paul is not negating full-time ministry by this, but in his case, it is clear that for the most part he preferred to be self-sufficient. We also need to take into account why he was happy not to receive a salary for his work in the Gospel. The culture he grew up in expected everyone to be self-sufficient. A matter of fact, Paul in his trade was so effective, one of his primary desires was seemingly to look after others as a way of living the Gospel (Acts 20:33-35). This of course is a big contrast to the Gospel that is preached by many today, more in line with self-help and improvement, rather than ministering the Gospel to the poor. Today we have ministers demanding their right to the tithe. If we, however, consider what Paul writes in his epistle to Timothy, true Gospel values are not linked to corrupt people who are only interested in financial gain (1 Timothy 6:5).

As a matter of fact, you would be very hard pressed to find any scripture to support the idea that the Gospel can be used as a tool to launch a person into financial prosperity. We also need to consider the fact that if collections are referred to in scripture, whether due to famine or any kind of recent disaster, it does not generally infer that the support is going directly to a church, but rather to the poor and needy. Scripture does not indicate that we are not allowed to prosper; however, a portion of the increase is indeed for the Lord, as shown in 1 Corinthians 16: 1-3. Something was laid aside at the beginning of the week to support the Saints in need, not the local church. An important point to add, this collection is not evidence of any type of tithing in scripture. Furthermore, depending on the translation of the Bible used, 'as he may prosper', may also be translated as 'in keeping with income'. We do not have any evidence in the New Testament of set percentages used for giving and certainly, clearly not in any of the letters from Paul. Tithing from the very nature of its definition had a set percentage. It was the law. If you had orchards, vineyards, lands and livestock this meant you. Yet there is no distinction or classification of any type in relation to the model of tithing in the new covenant. You only have the concept of free-will giving which was a percentage in keeping with your income and more importantly what a person desired to give in their heart. I decided to use the NIV, for this quote includes more emphasis using the word compulsion.

⁷ Each of you should give what you have decided in your heart to give, not reluctantly or under compulsion, for God loves a cheerful giver'. 2 Corinthians 9:7 (NIV)

This forms the very basis and nature of giving in the New Covenant. Paul instructed the high priest of the household within the realms of the new covenant and the priesthood of all believers, to give in keeping with their income; furthermore, to give according to the heart. The heart has a percentage in mind according to the means which are available. You cannot attach any kind of tithe percentage to that. Tithe means tenth, and there can be no squabbling regarding that definition. The other thing that weighs heavily is the word 'reluctance'. You either give cheerfully or not at all. Tithing did not require a happy face with a giving spirit, it was the law and if the Jews were in the category requiring the tithe, then they had to give the set percentage. It was the law! Another very important key word to digest is the word 'compulsion'. Tithing was not a matter of compulsion, or feeling compulsion to do something – it was a legal requirement devoid of feeling. Paul is very clear with this and I would like you to think how many times you have sat in church feeling compulsion to give, because the person at the front was indicating that you have a requirement to do so, whether tithe or free-will offering. The Apostle Paul had the credentials, did not mince his words and set it out pretty straight. Perhaps following the teachings of the Apostle Paul may indeed ensure for better provision, especially in view of serving under a better covenant with better promises under Grace by faith.

The Church loves to pull percentages out of the sky, especially if there are financial targets to be met, which leads us on to relative proportions. If you are required to give according to Paul in keeping with your income, then it is quite clear that Paul understood the concept of relative proportions well. Relative proportions throw up a very interesting fact. If a person is financially well off and follows the Old Testament legal tithe system in the new covenant, then just paying 10% of their income does not really make a big dent anywhere. If you are a low income household trying to balance the books and a legalistic tithe is demanded, it becomes a massive burden to balance the books and to try and stay out of ever growing debt. In both these extremes it is not difficult to work out that according to relative proportion, some should be giving significantly more than the 10%, whereas others should be giving significantly less, or indeed be provided for by the church. When a person is struggling enough, the best the church may do is tell them to give themselves out of debt, by increasing their offerings to the church, and that God can do more with the 90% than they can with the extra 10%. This is not common sense, it does not glorify God and it is stealing from the very poor people the Gospel (Good News) was for. Equally, as the high priest of one's own household, it is the family that should come first in the domestic church. As the apostle Paul writes to Timothy that neglecting one's own household is akin to denying the faith, making a person worse than an unbeliever (1 Timothy 5:8)! Most unbelievers look after their own! Why would people under the feeling of compulsion decide to do any differently? After all, this was the body of Christ Paul was talking to, not the world. The book of Proverbs even informs us that a good man leaves an inheritance even to his children's children (Proverbs 13:22).

The principle of the tithe is not always a financial cut off point, as more is often required. When church leaders start moving away from the law of tithing, something else sometimes starts to creep in. Although finally claiming that tithing is the law, they then insist that under a better covenant with better promises that the 10% should thus be the starting point of giving, or for better words 'A minimum standard'. One can clearly see the motive behind this teaching, which also does not fall in line with any theological discussions in this chapter, neither in scripture. Other ministers decide that instead of the tithe of 10%, the New Testament requires at least 100 %. The book of Acts will frequently be misquoted to encourage a congregant to give all their income and savings. In other words, the early believers placed in certain cases all they had at the Apostles feet. However, this does not take into account that it was for the redistribution of wealth amongst all those who were in need i.e.: 'The Poor'! This was done so that no one was left in need! The Church was and is still 'The body of Christ and People of God'! In Acts the Church was in its infancy and under persecution. Furthermore, there were no church buildings to maintain or ministers on the payroll. Unless the leadership want to supply all the needs of the congregation, this strategy has no scriptural basis! This is when the all-important background and context puts things into perspective. Plundering the congregation of all they have, based on Church history and Parables being taken out of context is not a pre-requisite for church growth. Congregants are not in sin if they are saving up for their retirement. Currently in the UK people will have to work till 67 years of age before they qualify for the pension they have paid into, even for those in jobs that require sound physical fitness and health. If you are a church leader, can I encourage you to use the principles set down by the apostle Paul of free-will offerings? We can preach all the sermons about Christ setting us free from the shackles, only to replace them with a new set of shackles rooted in legalism. This is everything Paul warned us about. Instead, could I encourage you to use God's standard of New Covenant giving? We can't go wrong if we use his divine principles. These divine principles worked when the Christian faith spread by the 12 to become the largest world religion. If you trust in him and put the new covenant to work for you, the financial needs of the body will be met by faith. Systems of control choke the life out of a congregation. Faith, hope and love will nurture a more positive environment.

This finally moves us on to the teachings of the Church, which in many respects were not based on sound doctrine, neither correctly dividing the word of truth. This chapter of course aligns itself to a more protestant stance. This formulates the yawning gap between exegesis and eisegesis. In exegesis study and analysis are required to come to an informed conclusion whereby the interpretations are formulated. Eisegesis is the exact opposite in that evidence is taken out of context with a list of presuppositions formulating conclusions to fit a particular view or stance that you already have. Any introduction in church teaching of the tithe system as a new covenant practice can only conform to the latter. The only New Covenant inference of tithing having taken place was the church in Jerusalem that continued to visit the temple, practise circumcision, honour the Sabbath, only physically consume kosher food or associate with those who practised the law. Yet this isn't evidenced, it is inferred. The Apostle Paul had much to say about this group of Jews who were not happy to mix with the Gentiles, therefore it is likely they were doing everything to the letter of the law (Acts 15 and 21). This would have been brought to an end during the destruction of the temple in 70 AD. Other than this inference, there is no evidence of tithing taking place in the early church and every New Covenant principle and teaching of the Apostle Paul shows us that the statute of tithing was made obsolete. His trade of tent-making with goat's hair was the same trade taught to Barnabas. It is important to realize that Jewish Rabbis were not full time and did not collect a wage as this was not fitting with their culture. They worked to earn a living and taught in the synagogue. Jewish Rabbis do the same today.

We only have mention of tithing some 200 years after Calvary by some objections that St Irenaeus was raising. Irenaeus wrote many sacred writings with untold volumes including 'Against Heresies' in the year 180 AD. Concerning tithing he clearly divided the old covenant from the new and placed tithing within the law and giving possessions for the Lord's purposes as a form of liberty in Christ in keeping with a new system of giving.

There was no mention of tithing in the first council at Nicea 326 AD, Constantinople in 381 AD, Chalcedon 451 AD, 2nd Constantinople 553 AD, 3rd Constantinople 681 AD, 2nd Nicea 787 AD, 4th Constantinople 869 AD or the Lateran Council in Rome in 1123 AD. (Kelly 2007)

Bishop Cyprian of Carthage is our first supporter for a possible move to this Old Testament system in the mid-3rd century (Croteau 2015). He was, however, unsuccessful in this and his views were only limited to his own sphere of influence. He felt the clergy should possibly be fully supported in the same way as the Levites were sustained in the Old Covenant. Whether he was attempting to have it fully instituted or if he was making a simple comparison is unclear. Clarke points out that this attempt of introduction does also dispel the myth that tithing had been common place. Cyprian was also an advocate of the tithe being the minimum standard of giving. (Clarke 1984 p 157). Cyprian, however, did have conflicting views with many others in the Church, especially on his views on the papacy and who qualified to administer the sacraments. This of course goes way beyond the tithe. He did, however, feel that the full time clergy should be supported by a tithe system.

When tithing was finally introduced it marked a time when New Covenant principles were being eroded. The introduction of the papacy and apostolic succession was a clear contrast to the principle of Priesthood of believers outlined in Hebrews. There was thus this new ruling class of clergy arising and a drastic change of theology. The order and structure of the clergy was closely resembling that of the High Priest, servants to the High Priest and common Levites for temple service. A higher caste system was put together and salvation was to be linked to the sacraments, with only specific people in the clergy allowed to administer them. The laity had been moved down to the bottom of the ladder! They would even need to go to the priest to be absolved of their sin in keeping with the High Priest in the Old Covenant. This was a picture of the watering down of the truth and doctrinal decline. Finally, the introduction of tithing to the Catholic Church marked one of the final stages of moving away from the principles of grace and rather a devotion to law. This new law was the power and authority of the Catholic Church which considered the magisterium (Popes, Cardinals and Bishops) to have the final say. The writings of the magisterium were the authority of the Church and considered God's word, even superseding the Bible. The Catholic Church is built on a man Peter, Cephas, 'the rock', (Matt 16:18-20) more so than the revelation that Peter had, that Jesus Christ was Lord and Messiah. The erosion of New Covenant principles happened over periods of time to resemble the authority of man, and man's ideas. Man's ideas were reverting back to the notion that a large structure was the church. This large structure would have been buildings called Cathedrals, where the bishop would have his seat or throne. These structures required money to build, money to maintain, furthermore the upkeep of a full time clergy. The understanding of our body as the temples of the Holy Spirit and Priesthood of all believers (Hebrews 7:5, 12, 18) (Laity) had been completely eradicated. Paul's writings make it clear that our body is the temple of the Holy Spirit who lives in us and that we in ourselves are not our own (1 Corinthians 6:19).

The tithe historically only makes a more formal appearance as a divine ordinance and merely an obligation of conscience and legislated in the bishop's letters at the assembly of Tours in 567 and the Canons of the Council of Macon in 585. This was of course based on Old Testament Priesthood. These Councils put tithing on regional church decrees, with excommunication of the body if not followed. It wasn't, however, civilly enforced until the Catholic Church had more political power so therefore difficult to fully control. The civil law enforcement then came into force between 774 - 777 during the reign of the Frankish King Charlemagne, whose sphere of influence also included northern Italy and Rome. The Pope at the time convinced Charlemagne to enforce agricultural tithing by quoting the Mosaic Law. If we look at the Catholic Church today, I can safely say that I have never heard a Catholic specifically talking about 'the tithe', although it was introduced by the Catholic Church. Some conservative Catholic Churches in Africa may, however, still practise this. One of the primary reasons the reformation gained so much popularity was because of the hate of the Papacy following the council of Trent, selling of indulgences for the purpose of freeing oneself and family members from purgatory. The hate for the tithe system of the day also fuelled this resistance. Martin Luther hated indulgences and was not a fan of the tithe system. The original reformers correctly divided the word of truth and formally stepped away from this teaching. Most Evangelical denominations include tithing in their church teaching and many use it as a pre-requisite to church membership. Why do Evangelical churches that claim to try and model themselves on the early church the best they can resurrect this ancient practice? The reformation did so much to enable the common man to be able to read the Bible and the power of the knowledge of God's word was once more in the hands of the people. Yet again, ever since especially 1870 the philosophy of tithing seems to have taken hold in the churches once more. Ironically, the practice of tithing can only be found in Evangelical churches and some other sub-sections of Christianity. Doctrinally speaking, paying tithes in the New Covenant makes as much sense as an evangelical attempting to gain access to God through the clergy, in other words – a priest officiating at the altar. This is in fact counter reformational and is not aligned with the system of the Priesthood of all believers.

References and Further Reading

Barker William, The Adages of Erasmus 1946; Translation by William Barker, University of Toronto Press, 2001
Bryan Alton The New Compass Bible Dictionary, Zondervan Publishing House, 1974 Clarke G.W.
The Letters of St Cyprian of Carthage, Ancient Christian Writers 43, Newman Press, 1984
Bulman Mary, Social affairs Correspondent, Food bank use in UK reaches highest rate on record as benefits fail to cover basic costs, Independent, 2018
Croteau David A, Perspectives on Tithing, 4 Views, B&H Group, 2011
Croteau David A, You mean I don't have to tithe? A Deconstruction of Tithing and a Reconstruction of Post Tithe giving, Pickwick Publications, 2015
Duignan Brian, Encyclopedia Britannica, 1989
Hodder and Stoughton, Illustrated Bible Dictionary, Thomas Nelson Publishers, 1986
Huggler Justin, Compulsory income tax on Christians drives Germans away from Protestant and Catholic Churches, The Telegraph, London 30th January 2015
Irenaeus, Against Heresies, Chapter 18, Concerning Tithing: Reviewing Scripture in Context 168 Sacrifices and Oblations, and Those Who Truly Offer Them; 180 AD, Anonymous
Jacobs Louis, The Jewish Religion: A Companion, Oxford University Press, 1995
Josephus Flavious, Antiquities of the Jews, iv. 240; Loeb ed. 93 AD Kelly Russell, Should the Church Teach Tithing? Writers Club Press, 2007
Kendall RT, Tithing: A call to Serious, Biblical Giving, Zondervan, 1982
KJV, King James Bible. Luther Martin, 'How Christians should regard Moses', August 27, 1525.
Meunier John, Sermon 'The Use of Money'. Methodist Publication. May 17th 2011 NIV, New International Version Bible. NKJV, New King James Bible.

Spurgeon, Charles. 'Entry for 'Tithes', Charles Spurgeon's Illustration Collection, 1870

Stendall Russell M, The Truth About Tithing, Life Sentence Publishing LLC, 2013

Talmud, Bava Batra 15a Tithing: Reviewing Scripture in Context 169

Talmud, Megillah 15a

Talmud, Megillah 17B Tosafot Ta'anit 9a, Commentary on the Talmud

Witherington Ben III, The Indelible Image, The Theological and Ethical Thought World of the New Testament, 2009

Wycliffe John, Tracts and Treatises of John de Wycliffe, D.D. with Selections and Translations from his Manuscripts, and Latin Works. Edited for the Wycliffe Society, with an Introductory Memoir, by the Rev. Robert Vaughan, D.D. London: Blackburn and Pardon, 1845

CAN A CHRISTIAN LOSE THEIR SALVATION?

This question addresses the doctrine of eternal security and is naturally one of the most frequently asked questions in Christianity. It has been an ongoing debate specifically between two opposing doctrines of salvation commonly known as Calvinism and Arminianism. The stance of Calvinism is of course rooted in the theological teachings of John Calvin (1509-1564) who was a leader of the Reformation. The counter theory is that of a Dutch theologian Jacobus Arminius (1560-1609) who formed the stance recognized today as Arminianism. Jacobus Arminius was originally a student of Calvinism, but had a radical change of mind after studying the book of Romans. I will now break down what Calvinists and Arminians believe in the next two paragraphs, then move on to a discussion of scripture.

Calvinism in itself relies on the supreme sovereignty of God, predestination, the depravity of man, unconditional election, limited atonement, irresistible grace and the perseverance of the saints. To put simply, all things are predetermined by the good pleasure of God's will. God is able to foreknow what is going to happen by his own planning. To the Calvinist, man is totally depraved and dead in his sin due to the Fall. He is thus unable to save himself and therefore this salvation needs to be initiated by God. Calvinists believe that God unconditionally chose (election) some people to be saved before the foundations of the world. This exempts the idea of man's future response. The elect, therefore, are chosen by God himself. In matters of atonement the belief is that Christ's atonement is limited to the elect. The Messiah, therefore died to only save those who were given to him (elected) by the Father. Christ, therefore, did not die for everyone, but only the elect with his atonement being wholly successful. God does extend his common grace to all of humanity: however, is not sufficient to save everyone. It is the belief that only by the irresistible grace that the elect can be drawn to salvation and allow an individual to be willing to respond. Grace in itself cannot be obstructed or resisted. Due to the depravity of man including their will, men are entirely unable to respond to God by their own volition, except for God's irresistible Grace. Perseverance of the saints is linked to the concept of eternal security. Those in the faith are likely to persevere in salvation due to the fact that God will see to it that no one will fall away. Believers are therefore secure in Christ as God will finish the work he started in them. There exists a strong Calvinist strand in most Evangelical churches and movements today.

(John Calvin 1509-1564)

Arminianism in contrast to Calvinism teaches that election is conditional, based on the foreknowledge of God, man's free will through prevenient grace to walk in line with God's salvation. This includes the belief of Christ's universal atonement, resistible grace and especially important to this discussion, salvation that can indeed be lost. This is different from Calvinism as God is believed to have limited his control in correspondence with man's freedom and response: furthermore, his decrees are considered to be associated with his foreknowledge of man's response to him. To the Arminian, man has inherited a corrupted and depraved nature due to the Fall of man. God removed the guilt of sin through prevenient grace. This means that the Holy spirit prepared a way for people to respond to the call of salvation. Through the process of conditional election man's act of free will is used to take God up on his offer of salvation. In matters of atonement Christ died for everyone. The death of Christ provided the means of salvation for all humanity. The atonement of Christ, however, is only put into effect by those who believe. Through prevenient grace, man is able to cooperate with God and respond in faith to salvation. By this Grace, God has removed the effects of Adam's sin, due to 'free will', also being able to resist God's Grace. All people have free will, because prevenient Grace is given to all men by the Holy Spirit, extending to all humanity. The Arminian is likely to insist that a person can lose their salvation by turning away from Grace as an act of their free will. Church tradition usually conforming to the Arminian tradition are Methodists, many Baptists, Salvation Army, Amish and Mennonites. You have classical Arminianism and naturally John Wesley (Methodist) was the main contributor to Wesleyan Arminianism.

Jacobus Arminius (1560-1609)

The reason why the debate between Calvinism and Arminianism is still raging today, is because one can see a Biblical foundation in both. The basis of the difficulty is also inherent in the nature of God's transcendence and attempting to deal with concepts that go way beyond our human comprehension or understanding.

This is the Church history in relation to the topic, now I would like to start digging into scripture in relation to these contrasting standpoints. There can exist this yawning gap between the two views, but it is a very important issue, especially when someone is evaluating their Christian walk. On a personal level this debate can also be internalized in the individual believer when fear comes to the forefront or even condemnation, whereby a person may start to begin to doubt their own salvation due to sin or spending a long time away from fellowship or the presence of God. Insecurity may also be thrown into the forefront if a person is then concerned about certain sins committed without knowing (unforgiveness) or a sudden burst of uncontrolled anger and a possible unexpected passing away of the individual. In an Arminian sense, since the sin may not have been repented of, would this lead to a loss of salvation? This struggle can be real for many people, especially if they have relied on testimonies of near death experiences resulting in a visit to Hell and then a sudden coming back to life and accompanied by a one more chance scenario. I would recommend everyone reads their Bible well and relies more on what God has given to us in scripture. One cannot deny a person's possible after-death experience, but equally when one has testimonies contrary to scripture or even blatantly contradicting other people's testimonies of similar events, then we do know that there may be a serious inconsistency. Reliability can only be achieved by trusting in God's word.

When coming from the standpoint of 'eternal security' and 'once saved always saved', I will be leaning closer to the Calvinist perspective. When people are introduced to Jesus Christ as their Lord and Saviour, they are brought into a relationship with the Father that guarantees their salvation which is indeed eternally secure. To bring clarity to the situation we need to fully realize what salvation really is. It is more than just simply saying a prayer to gain a pass or ticket to Heaven, and more than just making a decision for Christ. Salvation in itself should be characterized as a sovereign act of God by which an unregenerate sinner is washed by the blood of the lamb, renewed, and born again by the power of the Holy Spirit.

3'Jesus answered and said to him, "Most assuredly, I say to you, unless one is born 3/again, he cannot see the kingdom of God."John 3:3

" not by works of righteousness which we have done, but according to His mercy He saved us, through the washing of regeneration and renewing of the Holy Spirit". Titus 3:5

The new birth requires a person to be born again (regenerated). A person would have to lose this regeneration process in order to lose their salvation. We have no evidence in scripture that the new birth can be taken away. When the process of salvation has taken place, God has forgiven the sinner, renews their heart and places his new spirit within him. The original heart of stone will be removed from the person and be replaced by a heart of flesh:

[26] I will give you a new heart and put a new spirit within you; I will take the heart of stone out of your flesh and give you a heart of flesh'. Ezekiel 36:26

By the assistance of the Holy Spirit the newly saved individual is now able to walk in obedience to scripture:

[27] I will put My Spirit within you and cause you to walk in My statutes, and you will keep My judgments and do them'. Ezekiel 36:27

[26] For as the body without the spirit is dead, so faith without works is dead also'. James 2:26

There are a number of verses in the Bible that testify to this, and I won't be listing all of them, but it is evident that our salvation is secure by an act of God. The book of Romans especially hits this point home, that from the moment God chose us, we were justified in him, furthermore glorified as if already in his presence in heaven. There is eternal security everywhere communicated in this verse.

'Moreover whom He predestined, these He also called; whom He called, these He also justified; and whom He justified, these He also glorified'. Romans 8:30

In Romans Paul also asks some very revealing questions on the topic of 'once saved always saved', as he points out that it is God who justifies. No one can bring a charge against those God has chosen, neither can they condemn. It is not just Jesus who died, he was raised to life and sits on the right hand side of the Father interceding for us. No one can bring a charge against God's elect, as Christ himself is our advocate and the Holy Spirit is our witness. No one can condemn us, as the one who could have brought a charge took the punishment upon himself and the person in the heavenly courtroom who could condemn is both our advocate, judge and saviour.

[33]'Who shall bring a charge against God's elect? It is God who justifies. [34] Who is he who condemns? It is Christ who died, and furthermore is also risen, who is even at the right hand of God, who also makes intercession for us'. Romans 8: 33-34

If this were not sufficient, Paul reminds us that the same God who saved us, is the same God who will keep us. Once we are saved, we are therefore always saved and our salvation is completely eternally secure.

[38]'For I am persuaded that neither death nor life, nor angels nor principalities nor powers, nor things present nor things to come, [39] nor height nor depth, nor any other created thing, shall be able to separate us from the love of God which is in Christ Jesus our Lord'. Romans 8: 38-39

Scripture tells us that the Holy Spirit dwells within all believers and we are baptized into the Body of Christ. The concept of a person losing their salvation would also need to mean that the Holy Spirit would have to depart 'to lose his indwelling within us', and this would detach us from the Body of Christ. The Bible does not however give us this indication, nor does it give us an example of this taking place:

"But ye are not in the flesh, but in the Spirit, if so be that the

Spirit of God dwell in you. Now if any man have not the Spirit of Christ, he is none of his." Romans 8:9

"Even the Spirit of truth; whom the world cannot receive, because it seeth him not, neither knoweth him: but ye know him; for he dwelleth with you, and shall be in you." John 14:17

13 *'For by one Spirit are we all baptized into one body, whether we be Jews or Gentiles, whether we be bond or free; and have been all made to drink into one Spirit'.* 1 Corinthians 12:13

With this in mind, we also need to pay close attention to what the words 'eternal life', mean. If our lives are in Christ, then you have eternal life. Eternal effectively means just what it suggests. It is not something we are in one moment and immediately can lose the next. If it is there one day and gone the next, then effectively it would nullify scripture and indeed cheapen the process of Grace; Unmerited favour by God that was bought at a very high price for the very purpose of salvation and eternal security in him.

15 That whosoever believeth in him should not perish, but have eternal life'. John 3:15

In the previous chapter on tithing we already visited the account of the Rich Young Ruler who wanted to be justified by the things he had already done according to scripture. For example, in Matthew 19:16 he wanted to know how to inherit eternal life. Interestingly enough, the whole of chapter 19 is about the law and the account of the Rich Young Ruler has more to do with keeping the law, than giving possessions to the poor:

16'Now behold, one came and said to Him, "Good[a] Teacher, what good thing shall I do that I may have eternal life?"

17 So He said to him, [b]"Why do you call Me good? [c]No one is good but One, that is, God. But if you want to enter into life, keep the commandments."

[18] He said to Him, "Which ones?"

Jesus said, "'You shall not murder,' 'You shall not commit adultery,' 'You shall not steal,' 'You shall not bear false witness,' [19] 'Honour your father and your mother,' and, 'You shall love your neighbour as yourself.'"

[20] The young man said to Him, "All these things I have kept [a] from my youth. What do I still lack?"

[21] Jesus said to him, "If you want to be perfect, go, sell what you have and give to the poor, and you will have treasure in heaven; and come, follow Me."

[22] But when the young man heard that saying, he went away sorrowful, for he had great possessions'. Matthew 19:16-22

The moral of the account holds much for us still today, but in a New Covenant context, Jesus would have emphasized the necessity of believing in him to be granted eternal life, (Acts 16:31, 1 John 5:13) not following the rigorous law of keeping the 613 Mitzvah to satisfy the law. Salvation under the New Covenant can't be earned, but is given as a gift (Hebrews 8:6). This free gift can only be manifest in our lives through the person of Jesus. So in the same way, suggesting that we can be justified by not committing sin is a fallacy. Jesus knew the rich young ruler's problem was the love of money: this is why he mentioned it. Jesus knew that it is impossible to keep all the commandments: this is why God sent his son through the process of the incarnation to become a sin offering for us. The Jews considered themselves justified only by following 613 Mitzvah (laws) set down by the Torah and Talmud, as Judaism was a Religion of obedience to those statutes. In a new covenant sense, we cannot justify ourselves by our own acts: therefore, God provided a way. We are justified by the blood of Jesus and not by any works of man.

'For by grace are ye saved through faith; and that not of yourselves: it is *the gift of God: Not of works, lest any man should boast'.* Ephesians 2:8-9

Without Jesus we are hopelessly condemned by the law, but since we have him as our advocate and judge we are secure in him.

The strongest scriptural objections Arminians will raise to the concept to eternal security are found in Galatians 5:19-21, 1 Corinthians 6:9-11 and Ephesians 5:5. These read:

' Now the works of the flesh are manifest, which are these; *adultery, fornication, uncleanness, lasciviousness, Idolatry, witchcraft, hatred, variance, emulations, wrath, strife, seditions, heresies, envyings, murders, drunkenness, revellings, and such like: of the which I tell you before, as I have also told* you *in time past, that they which do such things shall not inherit the kingdom of God'.* Galatians 5:19-21

'Know ye not that the unrighteous shall not inherit the kingdom of God? Be not deceived: neither fornicators, nor idolaters, nor adulterers, nor effeminate, nor abusers of themselves with mankind, Nor thieves, nor covetous, nor drunkards, nor revilers, nor extortioners, shall inherit the kingdom of God. And such were some of you: but ye are washed, but ye are sanctified, but ye are justified in the name of the Lord Jesus, and by the Spirit of our God'.

1 Corinthians 6:9-10

'And walk in love, as Christ also hath loved us, and hath given himself for us an offering and a sacrifice to God for a sweet-smelling savour. But fornication, and all uncleanness, or

covetousness, let it not be once named among you, as becometh saints; neither filthiness, nor foolish talking, nor jesting, which are not convenient: but rather giving of thanks. For this ye know, that no whoremonger, nor unclean person, nor covetous man, who is an idolater, hath any inheritance in the kingdom of Christ and of God'. Ephesians 5:2-5

The importance of interpreting these verses correctly is being able to define the key word 'inheriting', in context. When one receives one's inheritance for instance as an heir it refers to obtaining reward from someone else. This does not mean 'entering', the Kingdom. Entering the Kingdom of God takes place when a person receives Christ as their Lord and Saviour. As a Christian I am living in the Kingdom of God to be revealed at a greater level when I pass on, not only after I have crossed to the other side. When viewing the passages above, these may refer to Christians who have indeed fallen into sin: therefore, they should not expect to live in fullness of joy and neither the blessing of God. It is likely the person would lose rewards at judgement day if the person knowingly continues in this sin. Another analogy taken from RT Kendall is that as a family member, I will always be my Father's son, but I can lose my inheritance and thereby lose a degree of my rewards. I can never, however, cease being my Father's son. (RT Kendall 'Once Saved Always Saved, 1983)

In conclusion. I can find no Biblical evidence that a Christian can lose their eternal salvation or to be unilluminated or un-regenerated by a departure of the Holy Spirit, neither prevented from 'entering', heaven. When a person is a Christian and truly follows Christ, there exists a desire not to sin in a life led by the Holy Spirit. Our walk may not be perfect, but this is why Christ died to become a ransom for many. Anything else one might suggest cheapens Grace and attempts to undo the redemptive power of the blood of Jesus. In closing I will finish this chapter by a promise from Jesus:

[7] My sheep hear My voice, and I know them, and they follow Me. [28] And I give them eternal life, and they shall never perish; neither shall anyone snatch them out of My hand'. John 10:27-28

References and Wider Reading

Bruce Demarest, The Cross and Salvation: The Doctrine of Salvation, Foundations of Evangelical Theology Series CROSSWAY, 2006
RT. Kendall, Once Saved Always Saved, 1983

WHAT HAPPENS WHEN WE DIE?

The next logical topic following the question of 'eternal security', is of course: what happens after a person passes away? Next to eternal security, this indeed comes up as one of the most frequently asked questions in Christianity. The answer to this is not clear cut. So many images from films or stories told to us as children simplify the situation pertaining to sitting on a fluffy cloud and playing a harp. However, there are a significant amount of differing views as to the timing of events following death and the passing into eternity, whether to Heaven or to Hell.

The Bible does not use allegory when talking about these places as they are real. The existence of these dimensions are not in question, although there are a number of theories people believe as to when a person passes on into eternity. There are beliefs of 'soul sleep', and that the person rests in their grave until the final judgment, others have a firm belief that instant judgment takes place immediately after death and being sent to their final destination. It is also evident that some people believe that the spirit man or the soul is brought to a temporary waiting place in the appearance of heaven or hell where they will be waiting for the final resurrection and judgement and the consequences or rewards that this brings. In this chapter I will be exploring what scripture actually says about life after death and attempt to follow a time line differentiating the subject of the afterlife in the old and new covenant, as they are very different.

I will first deal with the topic of 'soul sleep', or also known as 'conditional immortality'. This doctrine is especially prevalent amongst Jehovah Witnesses and Seventh Day Adventists. The theory simply believes that when people pass away, their physical bodies stay in the grave with the end of their conscious existence awaiting the resurrected body to be restored by God at the end of time. This view asserts, simply put, that when people die, their physical body ceases to function and the life force of the spirit is removed. This means that their conscious existence ends while they wait in the grave for a resurrected body restored by God at the end time. Their perspective is that human beings are not naturally immortal and do not survive, in any sense, after physical death. This Doctrine depends on the interpretation of some key scriptures. It is believed that both Sheol (Hebrew) and Hades (New Testament Greek) refer to the grave. Old Testament passages cited to support this stance are Ecclesiastes 3:19-21, 9:5, 12:7; Job 14:10-12 and Psalm 115:17. New Testament support can be found in Matthew 9:24; Mark 5:39; John 11:11-14; Acts 7:20; 1 Corinthians 15:51-52; 1 Thessalonians 4:13-17, and lastly Peter 3:4. The reason why these verses are significant is because those who have passed on, are referred to as 'asleep', or 'sleeping'. This is used as evidence of a non-existence in the form of 'soul sleep'. A perceived lack of existence of the soul and spirit unseparated from the body. The Greek term '*Koimao*', or '*Katheudo*', was a common term used for the word 'sleep'. It was only used by the Apostle Paul referring to people who had died in Christ. With the abundance of scripture in relation to these terms, of course doctrinally it cannot be ignored. However, it would be important to distinguish whether this is just in relation to the body or both the body and the soul. I think the appearance of both Moses and Elijah during the transfiguration quite easily puts the theory of 'soul sleep', to rest. I can confirm the pun was intended:

'Now after six days Jesus took Peter, James, and John his brother, led them up on a high mountain by themselves; and He was transfigured before them. His face shone like the sun, and His clothes became as white as the light. And behold, Moses and Elijah appeared to them, talking with Him'. Matthew 17:1-3

I think something very important to consider also within this topic is; how many types of death are there? This theory does not take into account two different types of death. You have the physical death and a spiritual death, because you have a body, soul and spirit:

'Now may ᵉthe God of peace Himselfᵈsanctify ᶻyou completely; and may your whole spirit, soul, and bodyᵉbe preserved blameless at the coming of our Lord Jesus Christ'. 1 Thessalonians 5:23

The spirit of a person that is not regenerated by Christ is dead. The spirit of humanity died when Adam and Eve through their sin took on the carnal nature. They had a body and a soul, but they were dead spiritually. They were born into this world but their spiritual self was not brought to life by the Holy Spirit and therefore incomplete. Ephesians chapter 2 verses 1-5 gives us a complete overview of becoming alive in Christ:

'Andᵃyou He made alive, ᵇwho were dead in trespasses and sins,ᶜin which you once walked according to the ᵈcourse of this world, according to ᵈthe prince of the power of the air, the spirit who now works in ᵉthe sons of disobedience, ᶠamong whom also we all once conducted ourselves in ᵍthe lusts of our

flesh, fulfilling the desires of the flesh and of the mind, and [h] were by nature children of wrath, just as the others. But God, [i] who is rich in mercy, because of His [j] great love with which He loved us, [k] even when we were dead in trespasses, [l] made us alive together with Christ (by grace you have been saved)', Ephesians 2: 1-5

Man is indeed made in the image and likeness of God, but without the new birth in Christ we are still spiritually dead in our sin. All descendants of Adam and Eve were born physically, but were dead spiritually. They were born into Adam's lost condition following the Fall. James 2:26 also shows us the difference between a live body and a dead spirit when speaking about faith without works:

'For as the body without the spirit is dead, so faith without works is dead also'. James 2:26

There is a time when we are born spiritually and we become a new creation in Christ. This is why in John chapter 3 when talking to Nicodemus, Jesus stresses the new birth. Let us look carefully at verses 1-12:

1 There was a man of the Pharisees named Nicodemus, a ruler of the Jews. 2 This man came to Jesus by night and said to Him, "Rabbi, we know that You are a teacher come from God; for no one can do these signs that You do unless God is with him." 3 Jesus answered and said to him, "Most assuredly, I say to you, unless one is born again, he cannot see the kingdom of God." 4 Nicodemus said to Him, "How can a man be born when he is old? Can he enter a second time into his mother's womb and be born?" 5 Jesus answered, "Most assuredly, I say to you, unless one is born of water and the Spirit, he cannot enter the kingdom of God. 6 That which is born of the flesh is flesh, and that which is born of the Spirit is spirit. 7 Do not marvel that I said to you, 'You must be

born again.' 8 The wind blows where it wishes, and you hear the sound of it, but cannot tell where it comes from and where it goes. So is everyone who is born of the Spirit." 9 Nicodemus answered and said to Him, "How can these things be?" 10 Jesus answered and said to him, "Are you the teacher of Israel, and do not know these things? 11 Most assuredly, I say to you, We speak what We know and testify what We have seen, and you do not receive Our witness. 12 If I have told you earthly things and you do not believe, how will you believe if I tell you heavenly things?
John 3:1-12

When viewing verse 5 Jesus says that 'unless one is born of water and the Spirit, he cannot enter the Kingdom of God', immediately the concept of water baptism and spirit baptism comes into play in many church doctrines. This is why the all-important context becomes so very crucial. When placing so much emphasis on one verse it is always imperative to read a number of verses before and after to get a full grasp of what is being said. A lot of Christians will take the water and the spirit aspect to mean that water baptism is essential for salvation. When the Bible speaks of the Kingdom of God it is something that starts at new birth leading to everlasting life, not specifically entry into Heaven. Furthermore, the context of this verse is in regard to being born again and not being able to enter the mother's womb for a second time, causing Nicodemus much confusion. In the context of water and birth it is clear that Jesus is referring not to baptism, but to a woman's waters breaking before giving birth. The physical birth by the mother is the first birth, the birth of the flesh. The second birth is being born of the spirit. A person's dead spirit inherited by Adam being brought to life by the Holy Spirit. This is the second birth, a spiritual one. This is why we must be born again to enter the Kingdom of God. This is the act of becoming saved. A person who is saved still has a body, soul and spirit, but the Holy Spirit comes to live inside that person, whereby we are empowered to live a life dead to the flesh, but alive in him. From the moment of the new birth spiritually, a person is born of God. Colossians 2:13 gives us a clearer picture:

'And you, being dead in your trespasses and the uncircumcision of your flesh, He has made alive together with Him, having forgiven you all trespasses', Colossians 2:13

A person who has been saved has been brought to life by the Holy Spirit. 1 Peter 1:13 also says:

'Blessed be the God and Father of our Lord Jesus Christ, who according to His abundant mercy has begotten us again to a living hope through the resurrection of Jesus Christ from the dead', 1 Peter 1:3

Notice the words 'begotten us again'. The word begotten ties into the new birth whereby we are living in hope through the resurrection of Christ. Everything that Jesus did in his death and resurrection was necessary for our new birth. We cannot be saved by ourselves, but only by what Jesus did for us. Jesus did everything required for this new birth to take place within you. We have been begotten through the Gospel, as Paul says in 1 Corinthians 4:15:

'For though you might have ten thousand instructors in Christ, yet you do not have many fathers; for in Christ Jesus I have begotten you through the gospel'. 1 Corinthians 4:15

The Gospel is the good news of Christ's death and resurrection. It is through trusting in this Gospel and what Jesus did, that we receive the new birth. This is why it is important to recognize also the two types of birth in the Bible. In John 1 the new birth in Christ is again made very clear:

[12]"But as many as received Him, to them He gave the [J]right to become children of God, to those who believe in His

name: *[13] who were born, not of blood, nor of the will of the flesh, nor of the will of man, but of God'.* John 1:12-13

I experienced the birth of both my children. When I stood there and they came into the world, they were covered in water and in blood. It is the similar analogy with us being born of the spirit, as we enter the new birth through the blood of Christ. True life only comes through Jesus. We were spiritually dead in our trespasses and sins before we became alive in Christ.

Returning to the question, what happens when we die, is that our soul departs to one of two locations. More evidence for the soul being separate from the body can be found in Genesis 35:18, when Rachel passes away after child birth, as her soul departed:

[18] 'And so it was, as her soul was departing (for she died), that she called his name [a] Ben-Oni; but his father called him [b] Benjamin'. Genesis 35:18

Now it is clear according to scripture that there are only two destinations the Bible speaks about concerning life after death and that is Heaven and Hell. No other variants are offered in scripture, especially in the New Covenant. The Old Covenant and literary Old Testament and the process of life after death was, however, slightly different. When we view what the Gospels say about Hell and Paradise it is also important to realize that we are dealing with literary New Testament, but Old Covenant. The New Covenant only comes into effect after the Death and Resurrection of Christ. Paradise was also a place referred to as 'Abraham's bosom'. The example of this is found in Luke 16:19-24 as Christ gives us an account. An important thing to notice is that he is not telling a story or parable. He is being very serious about these two clear destinations:

'There was a certain rich man who was clothed in purple and fine linen and fared sumptuously every day. 20 But there was a certain beggar named Lazarus, full of sores, who was laid at his gate, 21 desiring to be fed with the crumbs which fell from the rich man's table. Moreover, the dogs came and licked his sores. 22 So it was that the beggar died, and was carried by the angels to Abraham's bosom. The rich man also died and was buried. 23 And being in torments in Hades, he lifted up his eyes and saw Abraham afar off, and Lazarus in his bosom.

24 "Then he cried and said, 'Father Abraham, have mercy on me, and send Lazarus that he may dip the tip of his finger in water and cool my tongue; for I am tormented in this flame.' 25 But Abraham said, 'Son, remember that in your lifetime you received your good things, and likewise Lazarus evil things; but now he is comforted and you are tormented. 26 And besides all this, between us and you there is a great gulf fixed, so that those who want to pass from here to you cannot, nor can those from there pass to us.'

27 "Then he said, 'I beg you therefore, father, that you would send him to my father's house, 28 for I have five brothers, that he may testify to them, lest they also come to this place of torment.' 29 Abraham said to him, 'They have Moses and the prophets; let them hear them.' 30 And he said, 'No, father Abraham; but if one goes to them from the dead, they will repent.' 31 But he said to him, 'If they do not hear Moses and the prophets, neither will they be persuaded though one rise from the dead.' " Luke 16:19-31

It is interesting to discover that the Greek word 'Hades' is used in the New King James. The place of the dead in Judaism is referred to as the Hebrew word 'Sheol'. The good version of Sheol is also considered to be the same location as 'Abraham's bosom', or even 'paradise'. The Greek 'Hades' and the Hebrew 'Sheol' is not considered to be the actual word for Hell. It can be described as a place of waiting, which can indeed be a place of torment as described in vs 23 or a place of comfort as in 'Abraham's bosom', described as in verse 22, clearly as a place where the patriarch Abraham was. (Please notice, there is clearly no 'soul sleeping' going on) Furthermore, it was evident that between Hades (torments) and Sheol (Abraham's bosom) a great gulf was fixed so that those who wanted to pass from one side to the other were not able to. The rich man was reminded when he asked for Abraham to send word to his brothers, that following the Laws of Moses and the Prophets was indeed sufficient to escape the future place of torment. This also puts this account in an Old Covenant setting. It may be worth even referring to the current teachings of Judaism regarding life after death. It is also not clear cut. One of the two teachings of Judaism concerning life after death refer to Sheol as being a place that is Heaven for some and the appearance of Hell for others.

The destination after death of people before the crucifixion was not the way we understand heaven and hell today in the sense of the New Covenant. Christ had not yet died and been resurrected and the way was not yet open and free to be in Heaven. Therefore, Sheol/Hades was the waiting place. An example of a person going to 'Sheol' was Jonah, after he deliberately disobeyed God, refusing to preach to the people of Nineveh. God prepared a big fish to swallow him and take him to the place he wanted him to be. Although many a time it is taught that Jonah was somehow alive in the depths of the sea inside the fish, it is clear by the following verse that he had actually died as his body remained in the fish and his soul went to 'Sheol'.

"I called out to the Lord, out of my distress, and he answered me; out of the belly of Sheol I cried, and you heard my voice".
Jonah 2:2

Of course 3 days later he was spewed out by the fish and went on his way to preach a message of repentance to the hostile inhabitants of Nineveh. This in itself is a picture of the death and resurrection of Christ and clearly a raising from the dead orchestrated by God. A picture in an Old Testament sense, but an actual reality of things to come when the timeline merges into the New Covenant. Jesus said the following when rebuking the Pharisees for their lack of faith and the need to see signs, so he announces that no miracle will be given to them except for the sign of the prophet Jonah:

'Then some of the scribes and Pharisees answered, saying, "Teacher, we want to see a sign from You." But He answered and said to them, "An evil and adulterous generation seeks after a sign, and no sign will be given to it except the sign of the prophet Jonah. For as Jonah was three days and three nights in the belly of the great fish, so will the Son of Man be three days and three nights in the heart of the earth. The men of Nineveh will rise up in the judgment with this generation and condemn it, because they repented at the preaching of Jonah; and indeed a greater than Jonah is here'.

Matthew 12:38-41

These words by Jesus were fulfilled after he died and according to interpretation of scripture may indeed have changed the resting place of the dead, from Hades (torments) and Sheol (Abraham's bosom/paradise) to a different understanding of life after death in the sense of the New Covenant under the redemptive work of Christ. Since 'Hades' Greek and 'Sheol', (Hebrew) actually refers to the same place, it is important to understand that there was a good place of the dead (Abraham's bosom) and a bad place (Torments) with a massive gulf in-between that no one could cross. There has been much speculation as to what happened immediately after the death of Christ and the occurrences of the 3 days in-between his death and resurrection. One clue can be given to us by Peter informing us that Jesus immediately after his death proclaimed to the captives in prison, these were effectively those during the time of the Old Testament in the early stages of the book of Genesis that did not successfully make it onto the Ark due to disobedience. These words have been taken literally in the Apostles Creed repeated every Sunday in many liturgical churches, that Jesus descended into Hell. To be clear on a matter of definitions, some Bible translations do not differentiate between the words 'Hades' and 'Hell' or 'Sheol'. I am also not inclined to believe that the people Jesus preached to when he descended were let off the hook.

'For Christ also suffered once for sins, the righteous for the unrighteous, that he might bring us to God, being put to death in the flesh but made alive in the spirit, in which he went and proclaimed to the spirits in prison, because they formerly did not obey, when God's patience waited in the days of Noah, while the ark was being prepared, in which a few, that is, eight persons, were brought safely through water'. 1 Peter 3:18-20

Further Bible evidence that Jesus descended to the lower regions is found in Paul's letter to the Ephesians in chapter 4.

'Therefore He says: "When He ascended on high, He led captivity captive, And gave gifts to men." (Now this, "He ascended"—what does it mean but that He also [d] first descended into the lower parts of the earth? He who descended is also the One who ascended far above all the heavens, that He might fill all things.) Ephesians 4:8-10

Following this event that has posed as many questions as there are answers available, we see one of the strangest occurrences in scripture. Clearly following the death of Christ with the veil of the temple being ripped from top to bottom and the earthquake, graves were opened as a result and bodies of the saints that had fallen asleep were raised to life following Jesus' resurrection and appeared to many. When the Bible refers to the word 'saints', it clearly is referring to those people who held steadfast to God's law during the time of the Old Covenant. Their bodies that had fallen asleep were resurrected by the spirit of God and re-joined by their own soul and spirit and they appeared to many. This also marks a strong transition point in scripture, letting us know how the dynamics have changed and how life after death following this event has now changed forever. People were seemingly unable to fully enter Heaven yet, until the full redemptive power of the cross had done its work.

'Then, behold, the veil of the temple was torn in two from top to bottom; and the earth quaked, and the rocks were split, and the graves were opened; and many bodies of the saints who had fallen asleep were raised; and coming out of the graves after His resurrection, they went into the holy city and appeared to many'. Matthew 27:51-53

It comes as no surprise that the Centurion who presided over the death of Jesus proclaimed that he had come to the decision that they had just crucified the Son of God. Even one of the thieves being crucified next to Jesus who asked to be remembered when Jesus entered his Kingdom was told: 'today you will be with me in paradise' (Luke 23:42-43). This of course puts another spanner in the works for the 'soul sleep' theory. Since the full saving and redemptive power of the cross all that remains to figure out is what Hades/Sheol looks like now, since the saints in Abraham's bosom will have been taken out of that place. A possible answer can be given to us in Isaiah 5:14: I will use both the Amplified and the King James to cast more light on what has now happened to this realm of the dead.

'Therefore Sheol (the realm of the dead) has increased its appetite and opened its mouth beyond measure; And Jerusalem's splendor, her multitude, her [boisterous] uproar and her [drunken] revelers descend into it'. Isaiah 5:14 Amplified

'Therefore hell hath enlarged herself, and opened her mouth without measure: and their glory, and their multitude, and their pomp, and he that rejoiceth, shall descend into it'. Isaiah 5:14 King James

The 'realm of the dead', or Hell according to this scripture seems to have enlarged itself, with there no longer being as with Abraham's bosom (paradise) a large gulf in-between, as this section of Sheol is now empty and has been made one place. Half of Sheol was now available for enlargement as Christ had taken his own to be with himself to a new paradise. This is viewed by many to be the real and actual location of Hell as we would refer to it today. Paradise is however in a new location in the upper realms, as the Apostle Paul tells us in 2 Corinthians 12:2-4

'I know a man in Christ who fourteen years ago—whether in the body I do not know, or whether out of the body I do not know, God knows—such a one was caught up to the third heaven, How that he was caught up into paradise, and heard unspeakable words, which it is not lawful for a man to utter'. .2 Corinthians 12:2-4

Without a doubt these verses are teaching that Paradise is in the 3rd Heaven, a place the Apostle Paul went to as his spirit was caught up. This exceeds the revelations even that Peter had. Many of us are naturally very curious as to what Heaven is like and what people would be doing all day and this is why testimonies of people who have crossed to the other side are so popular, as people long for information. Paul is quite sober in his evaluation of the experience as he does not comment any detail, just that he in himself through the experience would have gathered a higher revelation. The all-important information that can be gathered from Paul is that he heard words that were unspeakable, furthermore not lawful for a man to utter. In all intents and purposes, he is clearly giving nothing away, neither is he giving us room for our imagination to go wild. In chapter 5 of 2nd Corinthians, Paul does however give us clear insight as to our current state. Although we are housed by our temporary bodies (tent), we have a new eternal building in heaven which is guaranteed. He also informs us that whilst our spirit/soul is still present with the body we are absent from the Lord. Being absent from the body of course, will mean that we will be present with the Lord.

'For we know that if our earthly house, this tent, is destroyed, we have a building from God, a house not made with hands, eternal in the heavens. 2 For in this we groan, earnestly desiring to be clothed with our habitation which is from heaven, 3 if indeed, having been clothed, we shall not be found naked. 4 For we who are in this tent groan, being burdened, not because we want to be unclothed, but further clothed, that mortality may be swallowed up by life. 5 Now He who has prepared us for this very thing is God, who also has given us the Spirit as a guarantee.

6 So we are always confident, knowing that while we are at home in the body we are absent from the Lord. 7 For we walk by faith, not by sight. 8 We are confident, yes, well pleased rather to be absent from the body and to be present with the Lord'. 2 Corinthians 5:6-8

Beyond this point it is safe to say scripturally that no eye has seen or ear heard, neither has it entered into the heart of man the things which God has prepared for them that love him (1 Corinthians 2:9). Not only is our eternity secure and safe in him, but we will not be able to fathom what God has prepared for us in Glory. This is of course in relation to the believer who is in Christ. For those who are not in Christ the Bible is clear, as their eternal destination will be Hell, the location described in Isaiah and many other verses of scripture. It is easy to assume that this is final. Scripture does make it clear that it is final, but only after the first death. Yes, there are two deaths. One location for those who have rejected Christ will be Hell after the first death, the other is the second death that leads after the judgement at the Great White Throne to a place which is called the 'Lake of Fire'. Revelation 20:11-15 informs us about this event where the dead who were not in Christ whether great or small stand before God and the 'Book of Life', is opened. They will be judged according to the deeds written in the book, with the sea, death and Hades having released the souls for judgement. After this the second death will take place when Death, Hades and anyone not found in the Book of Life will be thrown into the 'lake of fire'.

The Great White Throne Judgment

'Then I saw a great white throne and Him who sat on it, from whose face the earth and the heaven fled away. And there was found no place for them. 12 And I saw the dead, small and great, standing before God, and books were opened. And another book was opened, which is the Book of Life. And the dead were judged according to their works, by the things which were written in the books. 13 The sea gave up the dead who were in it, and Death and Hades delivered up the dead who were in them. And they were judged, each one according to his works. 14 Then Death and Hades were cast into the lake of fire. This is the second death. 15 And anyone not found written in the Book of Life was cast into the lake of fire'. Revelation 20:11-15

In conclusion and in view of these scriptures and eternal destiny, the final Judgement day is something everyone needs to be ready for. We have all fallen short of the Glory of God and not one of us are righteous. Therefore, it is difficult for many to feel worthy enough to be written in the 'Lamb's book of life'. Fortunately for the believer, it is not a matter of feeling, but of faith. I have explained this thoroughly in the previous chapter. We can only be justified and be pronounced 'not guilty', in his final judgement, because Jesus is both our advocate, judge and the Holy Spirit is our witness. We have been justified by faith alone and have peace with God through what Jesus Christ did for us on the cross (Romans 5:1). This judgement has already been made based on the perfect work performed at Calvary. We are declared righteous not by anything we have done, but through right standing (righteousness) with God, due to the fact that our punishment has already be borne by Jesus on the cross (Romans 8:1). Judgement day will therefore not be a day of condemnation for those who are found in Christ, but a day of final salvation.

DO PETS GO TO HEAVEN?

Following our questions on salvation and the afterlife in our two previous chapters, this is of course a very emotional question for many and is listed amongst the most frequently asked questions about Christianity. In Britain we are a nation of animal lovers. Many animal charities surpass charitable donations from the public compared with charities that are trying to save the life of one's fellow man domestically and internationally. It is interesting that our heart very often follows our giving. Many of our houses have pets which have become part of the family whether mammal, fish or reptile. To keep in tune with our passions, the Bible in fact does not really address the issue of keeping pets, let alone the salvation of them. One of the only recorded examples of someone keeping a pet as opposed to just being a shepherd is found in Nathan's parable to David, when he wanted to show King David the nature of his sin:

'Then the LORD sent Nathan to David. And he came to him, and said to him: "There were two men in one city, one rich and the other poor. 2 The rich man had exceedingly many flocks and herds. 3 But the poor man had nothing, except one little ewe lamb which he had bought and nourished; and it grew up together with him and with his children. It ate of his own food and drank from his own cup and lay in his bosom; and it was like a daughter to him. 4 And a traveller came to the rich man, who refused to take from his own flock and from his own herd to prepare one for the wayfaring man who had come to him; but he took the poor man's lamb and prepared it for the man who had come to him." 2 Samuel 12: 1-4

Another example in Mark 7:28 also informs us that dogs were

kept as pets during Jesus' day:

'And she answered and said to Him, "Yes, Lord, yet even the little dogs under the table eat from the children's crumbs." Mark 7:28

This does allow us to come to some form of conclusion about the use of animals in scripture, and that in some cases animals were kept as pets. Before delving into the deeper question we may first want to look at God's provision for animals. The general consensus in these verses, is that they are fed and not forgotten by God.

'He giveth to the beast his food, and to the young ravens which cry'. Psalm 147:9

'The young lions roar after their prey, and seek their meat from God'. Psalm 104:21

'Are not five sparrows sold for two pennies? Yet not one of them is forgotten by God. 7 And even the very hairs of your head are all numbered. So do not be afraid; you are worth more than many sparrows'. Luke 12:6

It is also clear however that God puts man above the animal kingdom, which we clearly see in Luke 12:6 in the 6th day of creation. Both man and animals were created on the 6th day. The whole reason why God cares for animals is probably also the reason why we have a desire to keep pets and nurture them. In Genesis 1:24-31 God gave us dominion and authority over the earth and told us to subdue it, implying the process of stewardship and care over his creation. A good steward looks after the affairs of the person who put them in charge.

'And God said, "Let the earth bring forth living creatures according to their kinds: livestock, land crawlers, and beasts of the earth according to their kinds." And it was so. 25 God made the beasts of the earth according to their kinds, the livestock according to their kinds, and everything that crawls upon the earth according to its kind. And God saw that it was good.

26 Then God said, "Let Us make man in Our image, after Our likeness, to rule over the fish of the sea and the birds of the air, over the livestock, and over all the earth itself and every creature that crawls upon it."

27 So God created man in His own image;
in the image of God He created him;
male and female He created them.

28 God blessed them and said to them, "Be fruitful and multiply, and fill the earth and subdue it; rule over the fish of the sea and the birds of the air and every creature that crawls upon the earth."

29Then God said, "Behold, I have given you every seed-bearing plant on the face of all the earth, and every tree whose fruit contains seed. They will be yours for food. 30 And to every beast of the earth and every bird of the air and every creature that crawls upon the earth—everything that has the breath of life in it—I have given every green plant for food." And it was so.

31 And God looked upon all that He had made, and indeed, it was very good.

And there was evening, and there was morning—the sixth day'. Genesis 1:24-31

If a person builds an animal enclosure in a Zoo or a kennel for dogs, then they are creating the environment for the animals, whereby the habitat is maintained and the animals are cared for. The animals then fully depend on the keeper to meet their needs in very much the same way that God created the world and creation depends on him to supply. One might suggest that maintaining a habitat for an animal is indeed a heavy responsibility and in some sense is modelling God, whereby there exists this small space a person is using to exercise their dominion hopefully with responsibility. It has been a parental strategy for a long time to use animals to teach children aspects of care and taking responsibility to improve their skills, empathy and character.

Pets do have much to give in companionship and many pets are fiercely loyal and can bring comfort to man. There is no going past the statement that a dog is indeed a man's best friend and will always celebrate the master's return back home with tail wagging and barking. So, if we take the responsibility of keeping a pet we need to provide for them and look after them. It is of course not wrong to love your pet, but as mentioned earlier, it is important to love humanity more. It is sad when people reject humanity and immerse themselves completely into the animal kingdom, even leaving their inheritance to their pets and not family or friends. Keeping this in mind, it is indeed Biblical to look after your animals:

'A righteous man regards the life of his animal, But the tender mercies of the wicked are cruel'. Proverbs 12:10

This approach, however, should not be taken too far as on the lop side of this argument, secular humanism has attempted to devalue the sanctity of life of humanity in favour of animals. These verses show that God cares for animals, but cares more for humanity as we are made in God's image and likeness. It is the image and likeness point that we need to take as the core value in tackling the idea of animals and salvation. There is no obvious teaching or evidence in scripture whether animals or pets actually have souls. We can only achieve any form of clarity on the topic by applying general Biblical principles and as mentioned before, these are almost all found in Genesis. It is clear that animals and humans have the 'breath of life', which makes them living beings, although it is very important to compare and contrast these verses as to which verses mention the 'breath of life' and which verse mentions 'became a living soul'.

'And the LORD God formed man of the dust of the ground, and breathed into his nostrils the breath of life; and man became a living soul'. Genesis 2:7

'Also, to every beast of the earth, to every bird of the air, and to everything that creeps on the earth, in which there is life, I have given every green herb for food"; and it was so'. Genesis 1:30

'And behold, I Myself am bringing floodwaters on the earth, to destroy from under heaven all flesh in which is the breath of life; everything that is on the earth shall die'. Genesis 6:17

'And they went into the ark to Noah, two by two, of all flesh in which is the breath of life'. Genesis 7:15

'All in whose nostrils was the breath of the spirit of life, all that was on the dry land, died'. Genesis 7:22

As you have seen and no doubt already know, humans are uniquely different from animals. We have a spiritual aspect to us which incorporates the soul and we reflect God in his image and likeness. Were animals to have a 'soul', then this would be of a different ranking and be subject to a different set of circumstances. It is likely these verses with the 'breath of life', hint to animals having an 'animated force' as opposed to an eternal soul. We have no indication in scripture of animals having an afterlife. They do not have a mind, will or emotions at the same level as humanity and do not worship, vote, use logic, apply conscience or make moral decisions or reflect on things they could have done better in the form of God given responsibility or act of repentance. Animals do not ask questions about the existence of God, neither do they have an understanding of the concept of truth. They do however have animal instincts that guide them in communication, nurture and survival. As animals do not carry the responsibility of committing sin, neither do they act on free will for the purpose of redemption. Animals are also not bound by a set of commandments. The Apostle Paul as always brings clarity to most questions:

'But God gives it a body just as He wished, and to each of the seeds a body of its own. 39 All flesh is not the same flesh, but there is one flesh of men, and another flesh of beasts, and another flesh of birds, and another of fish. 40 There are also heavenly bodies and earthly bodies, but the glory of the heavenly is one, and the glory of the earthly is another. 41 There is one glory of the sun, and another glory of the moon, and another glory of the stars; for star differs from star in glory'. 1 Corinthians 15:38-41

In these verses Paul makes it clear that both animals and humans have different types of flesh and in verses 48-49 of the same chapter he spoke of humanity having resurrected bodies. There is no mention of the animal kingdom receiving the blessings of the atoning work of Christ. There is of course a lack of information in regard to animals facing judgement as humans do in Romans 2: 6-10. If there is no expectation of judgement and hell, then it is quite clear that heaven can also be taken out of the equation.

If we look to the wisdom of King Solomon, Ecclesiastes may indeed provide a degree of clarity. The key verse in this book is usually 'nothing being new under the sun', although the concept of humans and animals in the afterlife is mentioned:

'All go to the same place. All came from the dust and all return to the dust. 21 Who knows that the breath of man ascends upward and the breath of the beast descends downward to the earth? 22 I have seen that nothing is better than that man should be happy in his activities, for that is his lot. For who will bring him to see what will occur after him'? Ecclesiastes 3:20-22

This verse seems to indeed indicate that animals do have a type of 'breath' (spirit), but makes it also clear that they have a different destination. The indication is clear that the human 'breath of man' ascends upward and the 'breath' of the beast downward to the earth. Most things pertaining to the earth become earth once again. Solomon also starts vs 21 indicating that 'who knows'?

In conclusion, there are likely to be animals during the time when there will be a new heaven and earth, as indicated in Revelation 21:1, but one would need to apply 'special revelation', on behalf of this question to place animals in heaven or paradise and equally place on them the burden of the same level of responsibility as humanity. We can scripturally place animals in the millennial rule of Christ on earth, but anything else is conjecture. *'The wolf also shall dwell with the lamb, The leopard shall lie down with the young goat, The calf and the young lion and the fatling together; And a little child shall lead them'.* Isaiah 11:6 If we decide to look to scripture to put animals in their rightful place, there are a number of ways the Bible offers an explanation as to how animals are to be viewed. The core value is to recognize that it is only humans who are made in God's image and likeness and have an eternal soul worthy of redemption. Animals can be seen to have a role in the earth by providing us with nourishment and food (Genesis 9:3) and can be put to work to benefit humanity (Exodus 23:12; James 3:7). Equally since the beginning of time they have been used for clothing, starting with God clothing Adam and Eve (Genesis 3:21) (Proverbs 27:26). Lastly animals can also serve as companions to man in the form of pets (2 Samuel 12:3) (Mark 7:28). The only way we can close this topic concerning seeing pets in heaven, is by pretty well coming to the same consensus Solomon did in Ecclesiastes; and that is: Who knows? Solomon did not have the benefit of the rest of the scriptures, but the silence on the issue may indeed indicate Biblically that it is not seen as a pressing issue scripturally.

Wider reading

Randy Alcorn, Heaven, TYNDALE HOUSE, 2004

WHY IS CHRISTIAN BAPTISM IMPORTANT?

Christian baptism is a much debated topic within the church and there are many different traditions surrounding it. It is also one of the most frequent questions asked in Christianity. Teachings of the church vary according to which denomination and the way it is practised, furthermore at what age it should be done will ignite fiery debates amongst all believers if they are passionate about the subject. The way to sift through the discussion is to differentiate between tradition and teachings of the church and what actually happened in scripture. There may seem a yawning gap in-between, but as you have so far discovered, scripture is all we have. It will come as no surprise that in some sections of Christianity it is the teaching and authority of the church and the documents that are held therein that even supersede scripture. The traditions of men should take a poor second place. The apostle Paul warns us against diluting Christ-given principles.

'Beware lest anyone cheat you through philosophy and empty deceit, according to the tradition of men, according to the basic principles of the world, and not according to Christ'.
Colossians 2:8

This of course can cause some confusion, as tradition can be a good thing but only if it is in keeping with the teachings of Christ. If we take baptism for instance, it translates from the Greek word '*Baptizein*', meaning 'to submerge in water', or 'immersed'. If something or someone is submerged, it goes completely under. The idea of pouring water on someone or simply sprinkling water on a person does not include the concept of being 'submerged'. Baptism is based on the Jewish tradition of being cleansed in a 'mikvah', with no sprinkling or pouring. The act of baptism re-enacts the believer's identification with Jesus' death, burial and resurrection. The believer is buried with Christ through baptism into death, so just in the same way as Christ was raised from the dead we also can live a new life.

'Or do you not know that all of us who have been baptized into Christ Jesus have been baptized into His death? 4 Therefore we have been buried with Him through baptism into death, so that as Christ was raised from the dead through the glory of the Father, so we too might walk in newness of life. 5 For if we have become united with Him in the likeness of His death, certainly we shall also be in the likeness of His resurrection'. Romans 6: 3-5

With this in mind, it is clear that full immersion baptism is the only practice of baptism that illustrates being buried with Christ and raised with him. The whole idea of sprinkling or pouring water onto people only started with the method of baptizing young infants. We see hints of this appearing in the writings of Augustine. This practice gained ground to induct a child into the Christian faith amongst a community of believers, welcoming them into the church. The Catholic church will baptize babies in order to cleanse them of 'original sin'. This is another contentious issue, as the sprinkling, pouring or even the full immersion of water does not cleanse us of 'original sin'. Only the blood of Jesus can do that in keeping with repentance and a full decision on behalf of the participant to go through the process of the new birth.

Baptism by the method of full immersion is and remains the most biblical practice of identity with Christ, but must not be seen as a prerequisite for salvation itself. When the thief asked Jesus to remember him when he entered his Kingdom, Jesus told him that he would be with him in paradise that day. No opportunity for Baptism arose with both of them nailed to a cross (Luke 23:42-43). Baptism therefore, should be seen as an act of obedience and public declaration of faith to oneself and others, identifying fully with Christ by faith. It was an outward testimony of the inward change in a person's life. This full submerging in water is the only way this radical change as a new creature in Christ can be demonstrated:

'Therefore if any man be in Christ, he is a new creature: old things are passed away; behold, all things are become new'. 2 Corinthians 5:17

We have no instances in scripture of infants being baptized, absolutely none. Only the practice of adult baptism exists in the Bible. The only way one can use scripture to read between the lines and evidence infant baptism is when Paul and Silas's jailer was converted, so he and his family were baptized. One would have to assume that his family would have had small infants to come to this conclusion:

'And at midnight Paul and Silas prayed, and sang praises unto God: and the prisoners heard them. 26 And suddenly there was a great earthquake, so that the foundations of the prison were shaken: and immediately all the doors were opened, and every one's bands were loosed. 27And the keeper of the prison awaking out of his sleep, and seeing the prison doors open, he drew out his sword, and would have killed himself, supposing that the prisoners had been fled. 28 But Paul cried with a loud voice, saying, Do thyself no harm: for we are all here. 29 Then he called for a light, and sprang in, and came trembling, and fell down before Paul and Silas, 30 And brought them out, and said, Sirs, what must I do to be saved?

31 And they said, Believe on the Lord Jesus Christ, and thou shalt be saved, and thy house. 32 And they spake unto him the word of the Lord, and to all that were in his house. 33

And he took them the same hour of the night, and washed their stripes; and was baptized, he and all his, straightway. 34 And when he had brought them into his house, he set meat before them, and rejoiced, believing in God with all his house'. Acts 15:25-34

We also have no evidence of any sacrament of confirmation taking place in scripture, as confirmation became an add on requirement by the church in the knowledge that the infant was not believing and become baptised, but being baptised by the parents only having to repeat the baptismal vows personally many years later to confirm that the person would hold their parent's faith as true. There was then naturally also a massive gap between the sprinkling of the water and the public confession of faith by a teenager to affirm and confirm the baptismal decision made by their next of kin. This is why in evangelical churches a baby dedication will take place in keeping with scripture and they will hold off until the child is old enough to come to their own faith in Christ. This is done to put it in the correct order of 'believing' and then being 'baptized' (Mark 16:16). This is why naturally any talk of confirmation becomes obsolete. Examples of baby dedications can be found in (Mark:10-16) (1 Samuel 1:27-28).

The importance of Christian baptism is recognized by two specific ordinances instituted by Jesus for the church. Before he ascended he gave his disciples instructions known to us as 'The Great Commission'.

'And Jesus came up and spoke to them, saying, "All authority has been given to Me in heaven and on earth. 19" Go therefore and make disciples of all the nations, baptizing them in the name of the Father and the Son and the Holy Spirit, 20 teaching them to observe all that I commanded you; and lo, I am with you always, even to the end of the age." Matthew 28:18-20

The Great commission was the specific mission and set of instructions specified for the church to make disciples and baptize the disciples they had made. This was to be done in all nations of the earth even to the end of the age. This was not a suggestion; it was a specific commandment. This baptism was different from the baptism of John the Baptist as John's baptism was a baptism of repentance and a preparation for the way of the Lord. New believer's baptism is, however, something different, as there is a far deeper significance. We see this communicated in Priscilla and Aquila's counselling to Apollos and Paul's visit to Ephesus:

'Now a Jew named Apollos, an Alexandrian by birth, an eloquent man, came to Ephesus; and he was mighty in the Scriptures. 25 This man had been instructed in the way of the Lord; and being fervent in spirit, he was speaking and teaching accurately the things concerning Jesus, being acquainted only with the baptism of John; 26 and he began to speak out boldly in the synagogue. But when Priscilla and Aquila heard him, they took him aside and explained to him the way of God more accurately. 27 And when he wanted to go across to Achaia, the brethren encouraged him and wrote to the disciples to welcome him; and when he had arrived, he greatly helped those who had believed through grace, 28 for he powerfully refuted the Jews in public, demonstrating by the Scriptures that Jesus was the Christ'. Acts 18:24-26

'It happened that while Apollos was at Corinth, Paul passed through the upper country and came to Ephesus, and found some disciples. 2 He said to them, "Did you receive the Holy Spirit when you believed?" And they said to him, "No, we have not even heard whether there is a Holy Spirit." 3 And he said, "Into what then were you baptized?" And they said, "Into John's baptism." 4 Paul said, "John baptized with the baptism of repentance, telling the people to believe in Him who was coming after him, that is, in Jesus." 5 When they

heard this, they were baptized in the name of the Lord Jesus. 6 And when Paul had laid his hands upon them, the Holy Spirit came on them, and they began speaking with tongues and prophesying. 7There were in all about twelve men.

8 And he entered the synagogue and continued speaking out boldly for three months, reasoning and persuading them about the kingdom of God. 9 But when some were becoming hardened and disobedient, speaking evil of the Way before the people, he withdrew from them and took away the disciples, reasoning daily in the school of Tyrannus. 10 This took place for two years, so that all who lived in Asia heard the word of the Lord, both Jews and Greeks'. Acts 19:1-7

Please notice that the act of Baptism is to be performed 'In the name of the Father, the Son and the Holy Spirit'; as in the Great Commission and Paul's visit to Ephesus. Through this process a person is welcomed into the fellowship of the Church. Please also notice, that amongst traditions of full immersion it can go a long time between a person's initial coming to Christ and then decision to follow on with their Christian walk by full immersion baptism. In scripture however we generally see that baptism immediately followed a person coming to Christ in a fairly short succession. There was little hanging around until a person finally decided if they were ready for that commitment. We see this with Philip and the Ethiopian Eunuch Acts 8:35-36. They wasted no time to get the baptism underway as soon as they came across some water along the road:

'Then Philip opened his mouth, and beginning from this Scripture he preached Jesus to him. 36 As they went along the road they came to some water; and the eunuch said, "Look! Water! What prevents me from being baptized?" 37 [And

Philip said, "If you believe with all your heart, you may." And he answered and said, "I believe that Jesus Christ is the Son of God."] 38 And he ordered the chariot to stop; and they both went down into the water, Philip as well as the eunuch, and he baptized him. 39 When they came up out of the water, the Spirit of the Lord snatched Philip away; and the eunuch no longer saw him, but went on his way rejoicing. 40 But Philip found himself at Azotus, and as he passed through he kept preaching the gospel to all the cities until he came to Caesarea'. Acts 8:35-36

In conclusion, it is clear from scripture that the only instances of baptism taking place was by manner of full immersion and only by those who were able to profess their faith with understanding in Jesus, which excludes infant baptism. Young children do not have a concept of right or wrong and therefore cannot fully understand the concept of repentance, let alone following one's Christian walk in believer's baptism. The Great Commission required the disciples to go into the world and make more disciples and to baptize them. You cannot make a baby a disciple. There was the practice in the Old Testament to dedicate babies to God and in this instance can be seen as appropriate, so the infant can ride on the parent's faith before being able to discern right from wrong and come to an actual knowledge of the saving power of Jesus. Baptism follows belief in Jesus having died for our sin and being resurrected on the third day, not being baptized and trying to figure it out many years later. The correct order is to believe and then be baptized in the manner of full immersion. A person is thus baptized into the Body of Christ which is the Church 'the people of God'.

'For by one Spirit we were all baptized into one body— whether Jews or Greeks, whether slaves or free—and have all been made to drink into one Spirit'. 1 Corinthians 12:13

Wider Reading

Believer's Baptism: Sign of the New Covenant in Christ, Edited By: Thomas R. Schreiner, Shawn D. Wright

New American Commentary Studies in Bible & Theology Series B&H BOOKS. 2007

WHAT DOES THE BIBLE SAY ABOUT THE TRINITY?

This is one of the major questions in regard to Christianity, what comprises Christianity and what sets Christianity apart from the definition of Christian Cults or even one of the main aspects that sets the faith apart from Judaism and Islam. It forms one of the most frequently asked questions in Christianity. The concept of the Triune God is exclusively linked to Christian beliefs, whether in the Nicene Creed 325 AD or in scripture itself. Before delving into this topic, I would first have to caution the need to put into practice the limited understanding we can apply to the Trinity, as I will be attempting to evidence the Trinity using finite means. It is impossible to describe an infinite God in finite means and with this understanding only are we capable of proceeding. God is infinitely greater than we are. He is omnipresent (everywhere simultaneously), omnipotent (all powerful), omnibenevolent (all loving), transcendent (outside space and time), imminent (active in the world today) and eternal.

The Biblical teaching of the Trinity is that the Father is God, the Son is God and that the Holy Spirit is God. This teaching is also in relation to monotheism (belief in one God) in that all three are God, but one God. This may not be in the realm of possibility for the human mind to understand, but that does not make it any less true. Before delving into scripture in detail, I would first like you to look at a diagram that may explain the concept of the Trinity in a way that we can understand, although I am not usually an enthusiast of reducing God to signs and symbols.

FATHER

is

is not

is not

GOD

is

is

SON

SPIRIT

is not

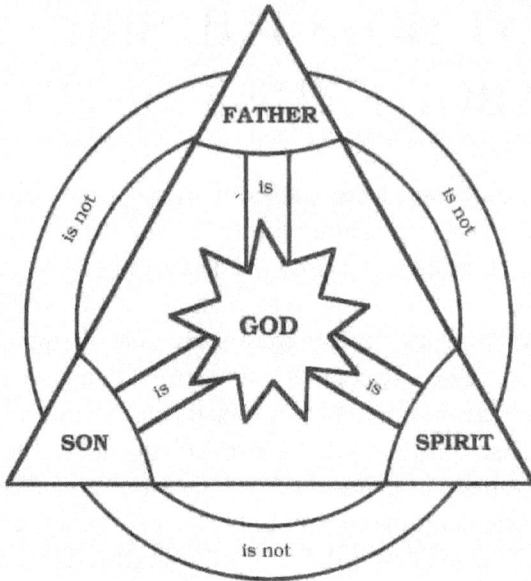

Romans 11:33-34 describes best the nature of the limits of our finite human understanding compared with the infinity of God:

'Oh, the depth of the riches both of the wisdom and knowledge of God! How unsearchable are His judgments and unfathomable His ways! For WHO HAS KNOWN THE MIND OF THE LORD, OR WHO BECAME HIS COUNSELOR'? Romans 11:33-34

We can neither fully define the Trinity; neither can we fully suggest what the relationship of the 3 persons of the Trinity are with one another. The Trinity is God existing in three Persons. The importance is also to recognize that there is no suggestion of three Gods here. You will not find the key word Trinity in scripture itself, but you have the concept of a Triune

God, coexisting with one another who are eternal and comprise one God. The Trinity is indeed a mystery, and viewed in a number of core beliefs.

- There is only one God
- God exists as three persons: Father, Son and Holy Spirit.
- Each of these three persons is distinct from the other two.
- Each of these three persons is fully God.
- There are not three individual Gods.

I will outline scriptures that dwell on the concept of one God in scripture first, before going further into the Trinity.

"Hear, O Israel: The LORD our God, the LORD is one! You shall love the LORD your God with all your heart, with all your soul, and with all your strength". Deuteronomy 6:4

This first scripture is incorporated in the most important prayer in Judaism called the 'Shema', due to the very nature of God being one. New Testament verses pertaining to God being one are:

'As concerning therefore the eating of those things that are offered in sacrifice unto idols, we know that an idol is nothing in the world, and that there is none other God but one'.

1 Corinthians 8:4

'Now a mediator is not a mediator of one, but God is one'. Galatians 3:20

'For there is one God and one Mediator between God and men, the Man Christ Jesus.' 1 Timothy 2:5

Although these New Testament scriptures specifically pertain to God being one, they also name Jesus as the mediator. All

Bible verses therefore need to be taken into account when researching a topic in the Bible. We cannot simply take a verse and dwell on it and ignore all others. The Bible tells us to 'rightly divide the word of truth' (2 Timothy 2:15), so here are the scriptures referring to God either as three or more than one. I will first start with the Old Testament verses:

'In the beginning God created the heavens and the earth. 2 The earth was formless and void, and darkness was over the surface of the deep, and the Spirit of God was moving over the surface of the waters'. Genesis 1: 1-2

'Then God said, "Let Us make man in Our image, according to Our likeness; and let them rule over the fish of the sea and over the birds of the sky and over the cattle and over all the earth, and over every creeping thing that creeps on the earth." Genesis 1:26

'Then the LORD God said, "Behold, the man has become like one of Us, to know good and evil. And now, lest he put out his hand and take also of the tree of life, and eat, and live forever" Genesis 3:22

'Come, let Us go down and there confuse their language, that they may not understand one another's speech." Genesis 11:7

'Also I heard the voice of the Lord, saying: "Whom shall I send, And who will go for Us?" Then I said, "Here am I! Send me." Isaiah 6:8

"Come near to Me, hear this: I have not spoken in secret from the beginning; From the time that it was, I was there. And now the Lord GOD and His Spirit Have sent Me'. Isaiah 48:16

'The Spirit of the Lord GOD is upon Me, Because the LORD has anointed Me To preach good tidings to the poor; He has sent Me to heal the broken-hearted, To proclaim liberty to the captives, And the opening of the prison to those

who are bound'; Isaiah 61:1

At this point it will be worth noting that in both Genesis and Isaiah the Hebrew plural noun *'Elohim'*, is used in combination with the pronoun 'us'. This denotes more than two equaling three. This is not complete proof in the Old Testament that 3 is implied, but definitely giving room for the explanation of the Trinity being visible in the Old Covenant. The Trinity is undeniable in the New Testament as described in the following verses.

'After being baptized, Jesus came up immediately from the water; and behold, the heavens were opened, and he saw the Spirit of God descending as a dove and lighting on Him, and behold, a voice out of the heavens said, "This is My beloved Son, in whom I am well-pleased." Matthew 3:16-17

'Go therefore and make disciples of all the nations, baptizing them in the name of the Father and of the Son and of the Holy Spirit', Matthew 28:19

'The grace of the Lord Jesus Christ, and the love of God, and the communion of the Holy Spirit be with you all. Amen'. 2 Corinthians 13:14

"I will ask the Father, and He will give you another Helper, that He may be with you forever; that is the Spirit of truth, whom the world cannot receive, because it does not see Him or know Him, but you know Him because He abides with you and will be in you'. John 14:16

I will use a number system identifying the Trinity in each of these verses. Following Jesus' Baptism as Jesus (1) comes up out of the water and the Spirit (2) as a dove descended upon him and a voice from heaven spoke 'this is my Son in whom I am well pleased' (3), is ample scriptural evidence of the Trinity, without the word Trinity having to be used. The Great Commission also commands us to make disciples and to baptize them in the name of the Father (1), the Son (2) and of the Holy Spirit (3). The apostle Paul clearly refers to the Trinity in his letter to the Corinthians. 'The grace of the Lord Jesus Christ (1), and the love of God (2) and the communion of the Holy Spirit (3) be with you all'. When Jesus (1) announces to the disciples that he will ask the Father (2) to send them the Helper (3), it was clear that he was referring to the promise of the Holy Spirit coming at Pentecost. This is why we refer to God as 'Triune'. We have three distinct persons in one God.

One of the points I made at the beginning of this chapter is that each distinct person of the Trinity is God.

1. We have God the Father being expressed in the following verses:

'Do not labour for the food which perishes, but for the food which endures to everlasting life, which the Son of Man will give you, because God the Father has set His seal on Him." John 6:27

'To all who are in Rome, beloved of God, called to be saints: Grace to you and peace from God our Father and the Lord Jesus Christ'. Romans 1:7

'Elect according to the foreknowledge of God the Father, in sanctification of the Spirit, for obedience and sprinkling of the blood of Jesus Christ: Grace to you and peace be multiplied'.

1 Peter 1:2

2. We have Jesus as the son of God expressed in these verses:

'In the beginning was the Word, and the Word was with God, and the Word was God'.

John 1:1

'And the Word became flesh and dwelt among us, and we beheld His glory, the glory as of the only begotten of the Father, full of grace and truth'. John 1:14

'Of whom are the fathers and from whom, according to the flesh, Christ came, who is over all, the eternally blessed God. Amen'. Romans 9:5

'But to the Son He says: "Your throne, O God, is forever and ever; A sceptre of righteousness is the sceptre of Your kingdom'. Hebrews 1:8

'And we know that the Son of God has come and has given us an understanding, that we may know Him who is true; and we are in Him who is true, in His Son Jesus Christ. This is the true God and eternal life'. 1 John 5:20

3. We have the Holy Spirit as God in the following verses:

'But Peter said, "Ananias, why has Satan filled your heart to lie to the Holy Spirit and to keep back some of the price of the land? 4"While it remained unsold, did it not remain your own? And after it was sold, was it not under your control? Why is it that you have conceived this deed in your heart? You have not lied to men but to God." Acts 5:3-4

'Do you not know that you are the temple of God and that the Spirit of God dwells in you'? 1 Corinthians 3:16

"I will ask the Father, and He will give you another Helper, that He may be with you forever; 17 that is the Spirit of truth, whom the world cannot receive, because it does not see Him or know Him, but you know Him because He abides with you and will be in you'. John 14:16

"But when He, the Spirit of truth, comes, He will guide you into all the truth; for He will not speak on His own initiative, but whatever He hears, He will speak; and He will disclose to

*you what is to come. 14"He will glorify Me, for He will take
of Mine and will disclose it to you. 15"All things that the
Father has are Mine; therefore I said that He takes of Mine
and will disclose it to you'.* John 16:13

It has been common-place to view the Holy Spirit simply as
this force or mystical type of energy, but the Holy Spirit is a
person and is described in masculine pronouns (he) and we
can see this all through scripture. The reasons to view the
Holy Spirit as a person are:

1. The Holy Spirit has the attributes of a person, as only
   a person can be grieved or lied to.
2. The Spirit performs the acts of a person, not a thing
   or force.
3. The Holy Spirit is treated like a person in every
   aspect.
4. The Holy Spirit is not described as 'it', but 'he'.
5. The Holy Spirit is God, therefore, by nature is
   personal as we have an imminent God.

It seems according to scripture that the separate persons in
the Trinity have differing roles, as scripture portrays the
Father as being the creator and ultimate first cause of the
universe coming into being. It is the Father who initiates the
following, including the incarnation and salvation:

*'Yet for us there is one God, the Father, of whom are all
things, and we for Him; and one Lord Jesus Christ, through
whom are all things, and through whom we live'.*

1 Corinthians 8:6

*"You are worthy, O Lord, To receive glory and honor and
power; For You created all things, And by Your will they exist
and were created."* Revelation 4:11

"For God so loved the world, that He gave His only begotten

Son, that whoever believes in Him shall not perish, but have eternal life. 17"For God did not send the Son into the world to judge the world, but that the world might be saved through Him'. John 3:16-17

The Son is portrayed as the individual through whom the Father performs creation and design of the Universe; furthermore, the divine revelation and salvation:

'Yet for us there is one God, the Father, of whom are all things, and we for Him; and one Lord Jesus Christ, through whom are all things, and through whom we live'.

1 Corinthians 8:6

'All things were made through Him, and without Him nothing was made that was made'. John 1:3

'For by Him all things were created, both in the heavens and on earth, visible and invisible, whether thrones or dominions or rulers or authorities—all things have been created through Him and for Him. 17He is before all things, and in Him all things hold together'. Colossians 1:16-17

'That is, that God was in Christ reconciling the world to Himself, not imputing their trespasses to them, and has committed to us the word of reconciliation'. 2 Corinthians 5:19

'And she will bring forth a Son, and you shall call His name JESUS, for He will save His people from their sins." Matthew 1:21

'Then they said to the woman, "Now we believe, not because of what you said, for we ourselves have heard Him and we know that this is indeed the Christ, the Saviour of the world." John 4:42

The Holy Spirit according to scripture shares in similar

capacity to the Son, the creation and maintenance of the world and everything that the Father does, he does by the power of the Holy Spirit.

As described at the beginning of this chapter, it is impossible to explain the Trinity using simple illustrations, as I would be attempting to use finite means to explain the complexity of infinity. The most helpful illustration I have managed to use with students in the past, is the analogy of H20. I am always careful to mention that I am not using modalism to liken the existence of the Trinity or compare a simple analogy to infinity. However, this method does help developing minds to understand. H20 as we understand it is water and can be manifest in solid, liquid and gas. This analogy only serves the purpose of demonstrating that one can be three, not that this is similar in the case of the Trinity. Any finite illustration one would attempt to use would never or could ever be accurate.

After analyzing all the Bible evidence on the Trinity it may be worth condensing everything to something more relatable and understandable in attempting to put the Father, Son and Holy Spirit in a framework of three but also one. In their most simple, elementary, basic and understandable form, with everything said and done, this is what scripture communicates:

1. The Father is the Creator
2. The Son is the Saviour
3. The Holy Spirit is the comforter and guide.

In conclusion, the Trinity has been the source of much argumentation in the history of the church. Naturally the Trinity, however, cannot be fully understood or realized, yet the existence of the Trinity cannot be denied or undone as I have demonstrated in scripture. There exists one God manifest in three persons. This is the Biblical Doctrine of the Trinity. We cannot de-construct the Trinity to find out how each personal component works scientifically in very much the same way as you cannot limit the awesomeness of God to testing in a test tube. The Trinity as a key word is not mentioned in scripture, but exists none the less in the Bible and church teaching throughout the ages. To successfully explain the three persons of God would put ourselves above him which is completely unsuitable for our human limitations, as none of us can claim to understand the mind of God nor to become his counsellor.

Wider Reading

Making Sense of the Trinity: Three Crucial Questions

By: Millard J. Erickson BAKER BOOKS, 2000

WHAT DOES THE BIBLE SAY ABOUT DRINKING ALCOHOL?

This is a big question that is not short of Bible evidence, yet is one of the most frequently asked questions in Christianity. Where you stand on the subject is very closely linked to upbringing and church culture in regard to the consumption of alcohol. Some see it as a perfectly normal choice of drink and accompaniment with a meal, others on the extreme fringes of Arminianism will suggest you are placing your soul on the line for merely visiting a place that serves the substance. This is why it has also made it into the top ten asked questions by Christians as the views on this can be so at the opposite end of the spectrum. I will carefully point to scripture so you can make up your own mind on the issue, as the Bible in no uncertain terms gives us plenty of evidence on the topic. My goal in this is not to give you the teaching, but to give you the text. In this very much two-sided argument, those who do not agree with drinking alcohol are likely to warm more to the latter part of this chapter. Vice versa of course for those who consider the consumption of alcohol as fine within reason.

If we research scripture, we will mostly see that wine is symbolically associated with blessing, celebration and the goodness of the Lord. In one of our previous chapters when we addressed the issue of the Old Testament Levitical Tithe system, the festival tithe was consumed in the presence of the Lord which was food and wine. It was a celebration with the Levites in keeping with one of the three tithes. Those who had produce from the land of Israel whether from orchards, fields animal flocks and wine, gathered to the place of the tent of meeting and the people celebrated the goodness of God and included the less fortunate in this occasion. We see this in Deuteronomy 14:24-27:

'But if the journey is too long for you, so that you are not able to carry the tithe, or if the place where the LORD your God chooses to put His name is too far from you, when the LORD your God has blessed you, 25 then you shall exchange it for money, take the money in your hand, and go to the place which the LORD your God chooses. 26 And you shall spend that money for whatever your heart desires: for oxen or sheep, for wine or similar drink, for whatever your heart desires; you shall eat there before the LORD your God, and you shall rejoice, you and your household. 27 You shall not forsake the Levite who is within your gates, for he has no part nor inheritance with you'. Deuteronomy 14:24-27

If I look specifically at verse 26 and move from the New King James to the King James it reads: *'And thou shalt bestow that money for whatsoever thy soul lusteth after, for oxen, or for sheep, or for wine, or for strong drink, or for whatsoever thy soul desireth: and thou shalt eat there before the LORD thy God, and thou shalt rejoice, thou, and thine household'.* Paying close attention to the words 'strong drink', it is difficult to get around the inclination to believe that it is not what it says it is. Modern day interpretations of any references to alcohol in the Bible will be to suggest that wine or beer was just no more than equivalent to grape juice or ginger beer, but scripture itself does not give us this indication, and neither does Jewish culture itself. Jewish culture did not share the practice of watering down wine like the Greeks and many other heritages surrounding it. I have heard of people suggesting in studies that the less alcohol there was in the wine, the better it was through a purification process; and that is what is referred to in verses that suggest drinking alcohol is acceptable. If we use this process to define the verses that condemn the negative effects of drinking alcohol leading to drunkenness and debauchery, then of course the context would naturally have to change. It becomes one of those situations whereby the stance drives the theology, instead of relying on what the text actually says. Associating wine with joy and gladness can also be found in the following verses:

'Go, eat your bread with joy, And drink your wine with a merry heart; For God has already accepted your works'. Ecclesiastes 9:7

'He causes the grass to grow for the cattle, And vegetation for the labor of man, So that he may bring forth food from the earth, And wine which makes man's heart glad, So that he may make his face glisten with oil, And food which sustains man's heart'. Psalm 104:14-15

'I will bring back the captives of My people Israel; They shall build the waste cities and inhabit them; They shall plant vineyards and drink wine from them; They shall also make gardens and eat fruit from them'. Amos 9:14

'Ho! Everyone who thirsts, Come to the waters; And you who have no money, Come, buy and eat. Yes, come, buy wine and milk Without money and without price'. Isaiah 55:1

Without you having to think particularly hard about it, I am sure you have come across the individual whose favourite passage in the Bible may include the Wedding at Cana in Galilee. For some people arguably one of the few passages they actually know, as it is Jesus' first miracle. At this event, the host at the reception ran out of wine and it is Jesus' mother who asks Jesus to intervene in the world by miraculous means. His first response is not to jump to the occasion as he seems to do so in a very reserved way. He asks the servants to bring six jars filled with water (jars usually used for ceremonial washing), then tells them to pass them to the master of ceremony. The jars of water miraculously get turned into wine. The point of this miracle is clearly seen in John 2:11, as his intervention in the natural order of things caused the disciples to put their faith in him. This was the main purpose of this miracle and the actual crux of what this passage is to teach us. Since alcohol is such a divisive subject however, it has become the main issue for most people. We are then immersed fully into the fermented wine versus grape juice paradigm.

As always, language in these matters becomes of utmost importance. The Greek word '*oinos*', is used in John which does not pertain to grape juice. It is fermented, therefore alcoholic. The word '*oinos*', is also the same word used when Paul warns us in Ephesians 5:18, not to get drunk on wine. You cannot get drunk on wine if it is not alcoholic, neither if it has only a slight fermentation and barely alcoholic. There is no historical or theological consistency justifying '*oinos*', as being grape juice. The Hebrew word '*yayin*', is fermented wine, '*tiyrosh'* is grape juice, but as the New Testament is written in Greek, we naturally do not see this. However, the context is clear if you compare the use of the word 'wine' in John and Ephesians. Furthermore, the context becomes even clearer when in John 2:10 the headwaiter gives his opinion on the wine tasting: *"Every man serves the good wine first, and when the people have drunk freely, then he serves the poorer wine; but you have kept the good wine until now."* This is a usual strategy at weddings to allow people to get tipsy on the best wine first and as the drinking time progresses they become less observant of the quality of the wine and the memories of the latter stages of the celebration. The context is clear. The wine is fermented and the best wine was left till last.

The wedding at Cana places the emphasis clearly on the first miracle of Christ. His disciples put their faith in him by the very nature of Jesus turning ordinary water into alcoholic wine. Jesus would not have done this if fermented drink

112

would be considered as sinful, disgusting or abhorrent, neither would God have permitted wine to be offered to him pertaining to tithes and offerings in the Old Testament. The account of the Wedding at Cana is as follows:

'On the third day there was a wedding in Cana of Galilee, and the mother of Jesus was there; 2 and both Jesus and His disciples were invited to the wedding. 3 When the wine ran out, the mother of Jesus said to Him, "They have no wine." 4 And Jesus said to her, "Woman, what does that have to do with us? My hour has not yet come." 5 His mother said to the servants, "Whatever He says to you, do it." 6 Now there were six stone water pots set there for the Jewish custom of purification, containing twenty or thirty gallons each. 7 Jesus said to them, "Fill the water pots with water." So they filled them up to the brim. 8 And He said to them, "Draw some out now and take it to the headwaiter." So they took it to him. 9 When the headwaiter tasted the water which had become wine, and did not know where it came from (but the servants who had drawn the water knew), the headwaiter called the bridegroom, 10 and said to him, "Every man serves the good wine first, and when the people have drunk freely, then he serves the poorer wine; but you have kept the good wine until now." 11 This beginning of His signs Jesus did in Cana of Galilee, and manifested His glory, and His disciples believed in Him. 12 'After this He went down to Capernaum, He and His mother and His brothers and His disciples; and they stayed there a few days'. John 2:1-11

Jesus as we know did not set himself apart from people or shut himself away from the community other than retiring to quiet places to pray. When John the Baptist (a man dressed in camel's hair and diet of locusts and honey) was imprisoned one could see moments of doubt as he sent a question to Jesus wanting to know if he was the person they were waiting for (Matt 11). After Jesus sends the message back answering a question with further statements, he puts John's mind at rest, reminding him of the blind seeing, lame walking, lepers being cleansed, deaf hearing, dead being raised and the poor having the Gospel being preached to them. There is also a clear difference that can be perceived between the limitations of the calling of John and the freedom in comparison with Jesus. His level of socialization with people as a whole can be seen by what Jesus conveyed in verses 18-19.

'For John came neither eating nor drinking, and they say, 'He has a demon.' 19 The Son of Man came eating and drinking, and they say, 'Look, a glutton and a winebibber, a friend of tax collectors and sinners!' But wisdom is justified by her children.' "Matthew 11:18-19

This serves as a reminder, that as Christians we can spend so much time devoting ourselves to holiness and right living which is commendable, but equally no longer reaching the lost as they do not seem worthy of our time, or simply attempting to live out the process of not being unequally yoked.

In Matthew 26:29 Jesus uses the word 'wine' again communicating that he would not be eating bread and drinking wine together with his disciples until he does so with them in the Kingdom of Heaven. Of course this pertains to the last supper and the Passover, and it was clear that any sharing of food and drink together had now come to an end with his crucifixion being short at hand. The Passover wine used at the Last Supper could have been 'tyrosh', unfermented grape juice, as the Passover required no leaven or yeast to be used as it was a symbol of sin, but only if we link it to the Passover bread. This substance is required for fermentation. In the Old Testament, God in Leviticus 23:5-6 and Exodus 12:8 lays down the requirement of bread without yeast. The New Testament uses the symbolism of leaven with sin in 1 Corinthians 5:8, Matthew 16:6 and Mark 8:15. Caution would still have to be advised with this interpretation however, as the leaven/yeast is only scripturally linked to the bread and not the wine in the Passover celebration.

*'But I say to you, I will not drink of this fruit of the vine from now on until that day when I drink it new with you in My Father's kingdom. "*Matthew 26:29

The last two pieces of evidence in regard to the right use of alcohol I would like to attribute to medicinal purposes. The Apostle Paul advises Timothy to drink wine for the stomach's sake. Wine can indeed be good for the stomach especially with red wine, as it is associated with better gut health. Some Doctors also suggest that red wine in reason is good for the heart. It is also clear that Paul was giving Timothy this advice as it was highly likely that the water he was subjected to in the area was not doing him much good, which is why people resorted to drinking wine as it was good for the stomach and saved him from the dangers of unclean water full of bacteria and contaminants.

'No longer drink only water, but use a little wine for your stomach's sake and your frequent infirmities'. 1 Timothy 5:23

Proverbs highlights something very interesting regarding the use of alcohol. Although it does not recommend its use for kings as it is associated with error and making bad judgement which we know strong drink will do. However, it is suggested for those who are already perishing. Verse 6 may be in defence of a person who is close to death indicating the use to be medicinal, much like the important Hospice movement that tries its best to make the passing moments of those who are terminally ill as painless as possible:

'It is not for kings, O Lemuel, It is not for kings to drink wine,

Nor for princes intoxicating drink; 5 Lest they drink and forget the law, And pervert the justice of all the afflicted. 6 Give strong drink to him who is perishing, And wine to those who are bitter of heart'. Proverbs 31: 4-6

The improper use of alcohol or the limiting permission of its use is also evident in scripture. We have a continuous reminder not to be given over to strong drink, whether in picking overseers for the church in the new covenant or the behaviour of the Levitical priesthood in the old covenant. From the introduction of the commands in Leviticus it can be presumed that Aaron and his sons had been given over to too much wine and had attempted to enter the divine presence of God in a state of intoxication. This is exactly the same forbiddance given about John the Baptist in Luke 1:15 as he was not allowed to drink anything that was fermented:

"Do not drink wine or intoxicating drink, you, nor your sons with you, when you go into the tabernacle of meeting, lest you die. It shall be a statute forever throughout your generations', Leviticus 10:9

In connection to this statute there were many who were commanded to separate themselves to the Lord in the form of a Nazirite vow. This included expressing one's special desire to draw close to God and to separate oneself from the comforts and pleasures of this world, which included fermented drink. There were a number of Nazirites in the Bible or people who had taken a Nazirite vow. We have Samson in Judges 13:5, John the Baptist in Luke 1:15 and possibly Paul in Acts 18:18, as he decided to cut his hair as a result of a temporary vow he had taken.

'he shall separate himself from wine and similar drink; he shall drink neither vinegar made from wine nor vinegar made from similar drink; neither shall he drink any grape juice, nor eat fresh grapes or raisins'. Numbers 6:3

In the case of Samson, he was the son of Manoah who was given strict instructions by an angel according to a Nazirite vow to also abstain from drink. His wife was barren and we see this interesting development of special ministries in relation to the barrenness of Sarah, Rebecca, Rachel, Hannah and Elizabeth. Elizabeth was the woman who miraculously gave birth to John the Baptist. This process of being set apart for the service of God has a strong emphasis in abstaining from alcohol. The instructions concerning what Monoah's wife must do in abstinence and how Samson is to be looked after and raised is very clear from these three verses in Judges:

'Now therefore, please be careful not to drink wine or similar drink, and not to eat anything unclean'. Judges 13:4

'And He said to me, 'Behold, you shall conceive and bear a son. Now drink no wine or similar drink, nor eat anything unclean, for the child shall be a Nazirite to God from the womb to the day of his death.' 'Judges 13:7

'She may not eat anything that comes from the vine, nor may she drink wine or similar drink, nor eat anything unclean. All that I commanded her let her observe." Judges 13:14

When the Hebrews were in the wilderness they were also going through a process of abstaining from certain foods and drink, as they were dependent on the miraculous supply of God who fed them over 40 years. They had no fields and clearly were not receiving the produce of any planted vineyards in the desert. So without any labour in the field or orchards, God supernaturally supplied bread from heaven and water from the rock, so that they would know that he was the Lord their God:

'You have not eaten bread, nor have you drunk wine or similar drink, that you may know that I am the LORD your God'. Deuteronomy 29:6

General instruction on not drinking to excess is clearly visible in scripture and not just in connection with a vow. The first part of this chapter has been in regard to the evidence of not abstaining from alcohol. The next part was connecting abstinence to a particular vow that God commanded. This last part is going to inform you about scripture that is blatant in warning against the abuse of alcohol and its consequences. We have many examples in scripture showing evidence how the abuse of alcohol can bring about disaster. Some of the patriarchs failed in this area as well. Noah built a vineyard and got blind drunk, putting himself in an unfortunate situation with his son (Genesis 9): and Lot after the destruction of Sodom and Gomorrah allowed his daughters to get him drunk, resulting in incest (Genesis 19). We would do well to follow the warnings of scripture on this topic:

'Wine is a mocker, Strong drink is a brawler, And whoever is led astray by it is not wise'. Proverbs 20:1

'It is not for kings, O Lemuel, It is not for kings to drink wine, Nor for princes intoxicating drink'; Proverbs 31:4

'Woe to those who rise early in the morning, That they may follow intoxicating drink; Who continue until night, till wine inflames them'! Isaiah 5:11

'Woe to men mighty at drinking wine, Woe to men valiant for mixing intoxicating drink', Isaiah 5:22

'Who has woe? Who has sorrow? Who has contentions? Who has complaining? Who has wounds without cause? Who has redness of eyes? 30 Those who linger long over wine, Those who go to taste mixed wine. 31 Do not look on the wine when it is red, When it sparkles in the cup, When it goes down smoothly; 32 At the last it bites like a serpent And stings like a viper. 33 Your eyes will see strange things And your mind will utter perverse things. 34 And you will be like one who lies down in the middle of the sea, Or like one who

lies down on the top of a mast. 35" They struck me, but I did not become ill; They beat me, but I did not know it. When shall I awake? I will seek another drink." Proverbs 23:29-35

Verse 34 is quite explicit as to how too much alcohol will affect a person's motor skills. Sailors who spent a lot of time at the top of the mast of a ship would suffer the maximum rolling effect of the boat. Later when they would try to walk on land, their body was still moving with the sea. It is clearly evident from these scriptures that God commands us to avoid drunkenness. The strongest position on this is to be found in the New Testament. Although I cannot find any evidence scripturally that drinking is completely wrong, it is very clear from the next verses that if you decide to drink, you would have to be one of the strictest people on drinking and the use of alcohol. Self-control is one of the Gifts of the spirit (Galatians 5:22), so it is clear that as Christians we would have to be the strictest people possible concerning the topic. If we need to ask the question, when is too much too much, then it is likely that person has already passed the boundary and pushed the limit in doing so in order to find out. By that time, it can often be too late. If you ask a drunk person if they are drunk, they are likely to tell you that they are still sober as alcohol affects judgement. This is why scripture warns those who are in authority like Kings or leaders in the church to very carefully consider the question. It is very clear that we cannot drink alcohol to excess and suggest we are doing so to the glory of God.

'And do not be drunk with wine, in which is dissipation; but be filled with the Spirit', Ephesians 5:18

Drunkenness is not just a sin, it can destroy lives and families through domestic abuse and neglect including self-loathing. Although alcohol is initially a stimulant, it mainly acts as a depressant. Many of us know very well the destructive power of overconsumption and are likely to know someone who either grew up with parents under the influence, or spouses. Equally, many people have been reduced to poverty and drank themselves into that position with family members having to be included in this misfortune. There are many things that are permissible for us, but clearly not all things are beneficial. Furthermore, if a person is an alcoholic, they will deny they are an alcoholic and refuse to admit that they may have a problem. This is why you have the old cliché during circle time in counselling meetings, whereby the person has to confess exactly what they are in order to be able to deal with the problem. It is important not to be brought under the power or brought into bondage by any substance.

'All things are lawful for me, but all things are not helpful. All things are lawful for me, but I will not be brought under the power of any'. 1 Corinthians 6:12

'While they promise them liberty, they themselves are the servants of corruption: for of whom a man is overcome, of the same is he brought in bondage'. 2 Peter 2:19

The other important thing to consider as a Christian, is not just the effect alcohol can have on us as individuals, but what it communicates to others. This is why during communion time, many churches will have non-alcoholic grape juice to prevent someone from stumbling who may have come from an alcoholic past. If we cause our brother/sister to stumble by our own actions, then have we really lived up to God's expectations in our actions?

'But take care that this liberty of yours does not somehow become a stumbling block to the weak. 10 For if someone sees you, who have knowledge, dining in an idol's temple, will not his conscience, if he is weak, be strengthened to eat things sacrificed to idols? 11 For through your knowledge he who is

weak is ruined, the brother for whose sake Christ died. 12 And so, by sinning against the brethren and wounding their conscience when it is weak, you sin against Christ. 13 Therefore, if food causes my brother to stumble, I will never eat meat again, so that I will not cause my brother to stumble'. 1 Corinthians 8:9-13

'Therefore, whether you eat or drink, or whatever you do, do all to the glory of God'. 1 Corinthians 10:31

In conclusion judging from Bible evidence, there are three ways we can look at the subject of alcohol. The first is to view alcohol as acceptable within reason. The second to view moderate consumption as useful for medicinal purposes. The third to completely abstain from drinking in view of the dangers of impeding judgement: furthermore, the possibility of it causing someone else to stumble. It is clear that God is specific in the avoidance of drunkenness as the Bible condemns this, especially the effects. We should not allow anything to master us, and alcohol when the temptation to drink to access is ever present, becomes addictive. Drinking to the glory of God with this in mind is not supported. However, with Jesus as our prime example it is also evident that at the Wedding at Cana he changed water into wine which was his first miracle. He drank wine on occasions. During the Bible era extensive work on sanitary conditions had not yet been mastered. Drinking water if it was not fresh from a good drinking source was risky and could often lead to stomach upsets and worse, very much the same in developing countries today. This is why people resorted to drinking wine, probably with low alcoholic value to avoid the bacteria and contaminants found in towns and villages. Timothy was instructed by Paul to avoid drinking water and resort to wine for the stomach's sake. It is unlikely the wine had the same alcoholic value we see today. From this study, we cannot substantiate the view that the Bible completely forbids people from drinking wine or beer or other drinks containing alcohol. The substance itself is not abhorrent or tainted by sin, otherwise it could not be offered to the Lord. Drunkenness, however, and the addiction to alcohol is something the Bible is very vocal to condemn. Measured drinking is not unhealthy or addictive. Some doctors will actually recommend drinking small glasses of red wine for the heart and stomach. We do have freedom in Christ to drink small quantities, but need to be on our guard and fully aware that the temptation of excess consumption can cause a person to sin and be a stumbling block to others. This is why for many Christians; abstinence is frequently the preferred option.

Wider Reading

God Is for the Alcoholic, By: Bernard Palmer MOODY PUBLISHERS, 1986

God the Son Incarnate: The Doctrine of Christ, By: Stephen J. Wellum, John S. Feinberg, Foundations of Evangelical Theology Series, CROSSWAY, 2016

WHAT DOES THE BIBLE SAY CONCERNING DIVORCE?

This is the final chapter in the book and again one of the most frequently asked questions in Christianity. Before explaining in detail what the Bible says about it, it may be important to go through a number of Biblical definitions of key words before continuing. Divorce cannot take place unless two people are married. The God ordained commitment for a man and woman to engage in sexual activity is within the marriage covenant. The Bible defines marriage as being between a man and a woman, which legally differs between many countries today, as same sex couples can legally marry and will be legally defined as the joining of two persons. Further to this conversation are the definitions of fornication and adultery. In order for adultery to take place, one or both of the people need to be married. The act of adultery breaks the marital covenant. Fornication is when sex takes place between a man and a woman outside the confines of marriage, which the Bible also does not support. It is my intention in this chapter as always, to mention the teachings of the church but to ask the all-important question as a whole - what does the text say? By this I mean not some examples in scripture, but all of the scripture to give us a complete picture of the heart of God on the issue.

As always, views on this topic are very closely linked to the teachings of the church. A number of denominations may interpret scripture differently. One need to look no further to acknowledge the massive gap in teaching between the Catholic Church and the Church of England on the topic of Divorce.

The Catholic Church will view marriage as a sacrament, furthermore not consider divorce ever taking place, even in the case of marital unfaithfulness. They would permit separation, but the two people would forever have to remain married. In the past people have been refused to take communion if they legally sought divorce. The only way a marriage can be brought to an end in Catholicism, is either by death or by annulment. An annulment usually is only granted in a shorter time period after marriage has taken place. Annulment basically means to be made zero, as if it never happened. This can only take place for one of three reasons. An annulment can firstly be granted, if the spouses did not know what they were doing when they took the wedding vows. It will secondly also become possible if one of the people getting married was having an affair with another, meaning that they could not have meant their wedding vows. The third and last reason given is the unusual case of the marriage not being consummated and thus two people not becoming one, as this is the physical act of marriage.

'So then, they are no longer two but one flesh. Therefore, what God has joined together, let not man separate. "Matthew 19:6

The very strict teaching of the Catholic Church will exclusively be linked to Mark 10:11.

'So He said to them, "Whoever divorces his wife and marries another commits adultery against her. Mark 10:11

The teaching of the Church of England and other evangelical churches is different, as it takes more of scripture into account instead of just dwelling on one verse. This is also where the all important aspect of Grace comes into the forefront. Jesus did say divorce was permitted if sexual immorality has taken place, thereby breaking the marriage covenant. This is why it is important to look to scripture and avoid the overreliance or dependence on one verse in the Bible and ignoring all others.

'But I say to you that whoever divorces his wife for any reason *except sexual immorality causes her to commit adultery; and whoever marries a woman who is divorced commits adultery'.* Matthew 5:32

This seeming exemption of 'marital unfaithfulness' as other translations use, can be understood as an 'exception clause', during the Jewish betrothal period. We need to remember that Jesus was speaking to the Jews and in Jewish custom a man and a woman were to consider themselves married after the period of 'betrothal' had begun, which is very different from our western culture of engagement. This betrothal period was so strict, that one would need to get a divorce to break the betrothal and some interpreters think this is what Jesus was referring to and not people who had actually been fully joined together as husband and wife.

If this was not regarding Jewish betrothal then Jesus therefore, clearly states that under certain circumstances, divorce is an option. Looking at the Greek for 'marital unfaithfulness', a lot more comes to light. The Greek word for this is *'porneia'*, which means 'fornication and all forms of illicit or unlawful sexual intercourse in general'. This could be that it simply means 'breaking faith', with one's partner rather than full on sexual involvement with someone else. It appears that the use of the word goes beyond covenant breaking, incompatibility or disloyalty. It is also interesting that the Greek word used for 'adultery', in this instance is the word *'moicheaia'*, emphasises the purity of the marriage bond. Jesus was clear about sexual involvement with others *'porneaia'*, breaking the covenant and he didn't merely restrict the sin to the act of adultery, but included all forms of sexual infidelity. Therefore, it may be that Jesus did permit divorce when any form of *'porneia'*, has been committed and not just *'moicheia'*. Others still may suggest that marital unfaithfulness may include abandonment in the bedroom whereby a spouse is not being honoured in that part of the covenant relationship. Jesus in Matthew 19:9 may have had remarriage in mind when using the words 'and marries another', as the exception clause applies. This, however, could only be in instants of the innocent party who has been sinned against, not for the person who perpetrated the act. It could be possible for the perpetrator of unfaithfulness to remarry, but we do not have any clear indication of that in the text:

'And I say to you, whoever divorces his wife, except for sexual immorality, and marries another, commits adultery; and whoever marries her who is divorced commits adultery."
Matthew 19:9

He reminded the multitude in Matthew, however, that during the old covenant, divorce was permitted due to the hardness of people's hearts and that it was not God's intention for this to take place in the beginning:

'He said to them, "Moses, because of the hardness of your hearts, permitted you to divorce your wives, but from the beginning it was not so'. Matthew 19:8

This view is clearly expressed in the Book of Malachi when God says that he hates divorce:

"For I hate divorce," says the LORD, the God of Israel'. Malachi 2:16

According to scripture, marriage is for life and not just a temporary arrangement. Matthew 19:6 confirms that two have become one in a covenant. This taken into account, it can also clearly be recognized that God realizes that when you have two imperfect individuals coming together, that there may be difficulties and that it may not work out. In the old covenant God put laws in place to protect mainly women from this situation:

"When a man takes a wife and marries her, and it happens

that she finds no favour in his eyes because he has found some indecency in her, and he writes her a certificate of divorce and puts it in her hand and sends her out from his house, 2 and she leaves his house and goes and becomes another man's wife, 3 and if the latter husband turns against her and writes her a certificate of divorce and puts it in her hand and sends her out of his house, or if the latter husband dies who took her to be his wife, 4 then her former husband who sent her away is not allowed to take her again to be his wife, since she has been defiled; for that is an abomination before the LORD, and you shall not bring sin on the land which the LORD your God gives you as an inheritance'. Deuteronomy 24:1-4

Some people interpret 1 Corinthians 7:15 as a further 'exception', permitting re-marriage to occur if an unbelieving spouse divorces someone practising the faith. The text is not specific in referring to re-marriage, but does include not having to continue in the marriage if the unbelieving spouse wants to take their leave. Still others again may suggest that abuse, whether toward a spouse or child is a sufficient reason to put this exemption into immediate effect, however, the text is again not clear on this.

'But if the unbeliever departs, let him depart; a brother or a sister is not under bondage in such cases. But God has called us to peace'. 1 Corinthians 7:15

No matter what the interpretation of any exception clause to divorce may be or what 'marital unfaithfulness' is actually defined as, it is important to note that it is a permission clause, not a requirement to act on it. A couple can still work through the pain of adultery through the Grace of God and learn to forgive and attempt to rebuild their union. In life we have been forgiven of all things through repentance and we owe it to one another to extend this same act of forgiveness.

'And be kind to one another, tender-hearted, forgiving one another, even as God in Christ forgave you'. Ephesians 4:32

It is when there exists this unrepentant state of perpetual sexual immorality when the realization sinks in that repentance has not occurred. This is when Matthew 19:19 may be applicable. It is wise after such an ordeal to remain single for a time and not to dive into another relationship in order to rest, heal and seek God's heart for your life. It is the pain, confusion and frustration many people experience which is the likely reason why God hates divorce. For many who experience divorce it becomes a more difficult ordeal than losing a loved one to an illness or accident. In the mourning process a person in most cases can overcome, bury the dead with earth and put the situation behind them. In the case of divorce, especially if children are involved, the same person can still be in your life forever and it will be difficult to deal with the hurt and rejection no matter the reason for the divorce taking place.

For clarity, if divorce takes place for any other reason than the reasons already mentioned, then if they remarry, then adultery has been committed. This leads us, however, to another segment of possible contention. One would need to ask the question if the remarriage is classified as the 'act of adultery', or a continued 'state of adultery', within that marriage. It could be argued that the process of the re-marriage procedure on the actual day it is taking place could be seen as adultery, not the aftermath of that decision.

In conclusion, divorce is only permissible under the clause of 'marital unfaithfulness' as referred to in the New Testament. In the Old Testament the law was clear. The punishment for adultery was death (Lev 20:10). However, as discovered in Deuteronomy 24:1-4, re-marriage is referred to after divorce. Scripture is clear in Malachi that God hates divorce. However, we have no examples in the Bible of God hating re-marriage or suggesting that re-marriage is not valid. This means that the ending of a second marriage would be as serious as ending the first, as in both instances it would mean that the marital vows have been broken between the man, woman and God. It is also clear that God permits divorce in the case of both abandonment and adultery, but this does not mean that this should be the first resort. There is much to be said for the Grace of God in both the decision to divorce or if a person is in a second marriage. It is best to reconcile instead of divorce as in the same way God through his son reconciled himself to us. Forgiveness is given to us freely, so we should also freely forgive (Colossians 3:13). This is, however, different if a spouse chooses to be abusive or continue in sexual unfaithfulness. Lastly there seems to be flexibility if a person is married to an unbelieving spouse, as the believer is not called to bondage, but to peace (1 Corinthians 7:15).

The best way to avoid divorce in the first place is to choose a spouse wisely and hopefully identify any shortcomings of the individual before the wedding takes place. This is why it is wise to first go to pre-marital counselling to identify differing views and character traits or even responses given in varied scenarios. Many a time the true nature of the individual will not be completely hidden before marriage and shortcomings will come to the forefront. If they slump into irrational jealousy, continuously claw at the need for being completely in control, are fast to anger, attempt to isolate you from family and friends, disrespect clear boundaries, are involved in substance abuse, bad with finances and have generally low moral values not in keeping with a spirit-filled Christian life, then the warning signs are clear. Uniting yourself by marriage to such an individual will not be fulfilling and there is no point assuming the person will change over time. God designed marriage to be a blessing, and when both spouses fulfil their assigned duty giving a hundred percent to one another; then the backbone of both the successful domestic family and prosperous church family is formed inclusive of a better society.

Wider Reading

Divorce & Remarriage: 4 views, Edited By: H. Wayne House
INTERVARSITY PRESS, 1990

OTHER BOOKS BY THE AUTHOR

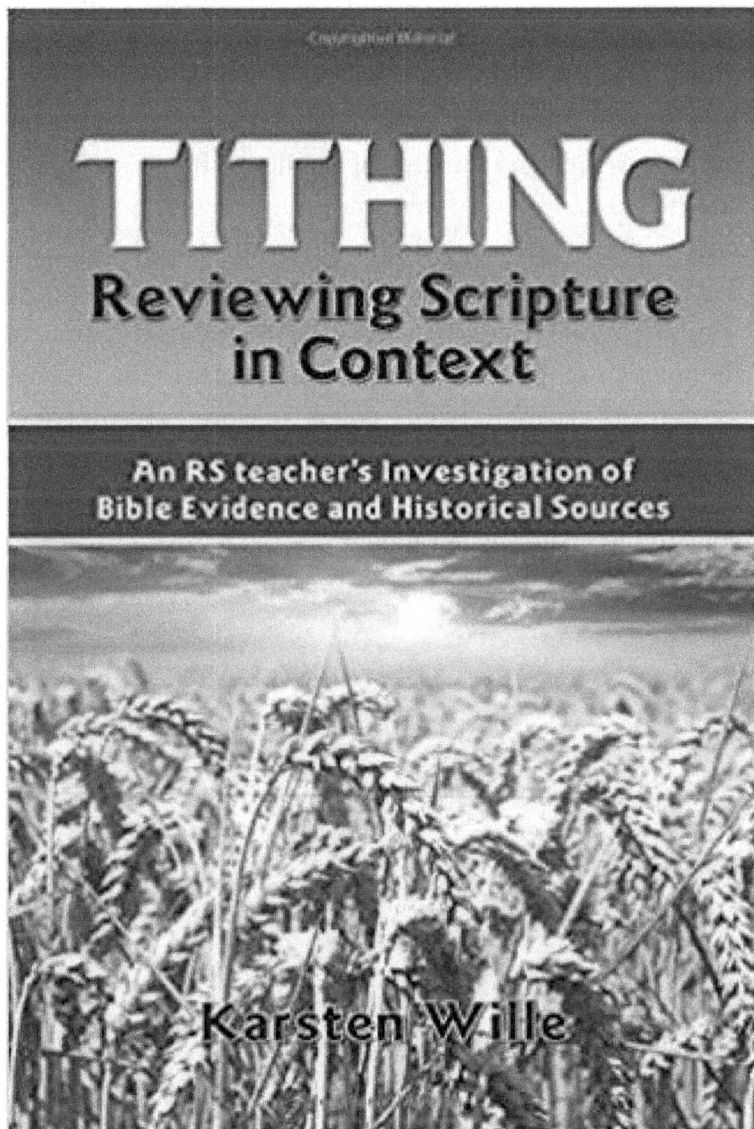

TITHING
Reviewing Scripture in Context

An RS teacher's Investigation of Bible Evidence and Historical Sources

Karsten Wille

This book analyses tithing in the context of Biblical scripture. Tithing is mentioned many times in the Bible and many theories have been developed over time especially concerning the possible need of giving a tenth of one's income in the New Testament Church. This subject has divided many people with a special focus on the Law as opposed to freewill giving. It is Karsten's intention to delve into scripture, commenting on the customs and cultures of the times they were written and the audiences they were meant to capture. Scripture is only useful if we rightly divide the word of truth, which is consequently only possible if we study ourselves approved (2 Timothy 2:15). Karsten summarizes all the main points of the study of scripture and context, then finalizes the findings in easy to navigate bullet points to form an overview, narrowing evidence into a systematic review. A clear picture of the subject arises, whereby you can determine your own conclusions regarding this topic.

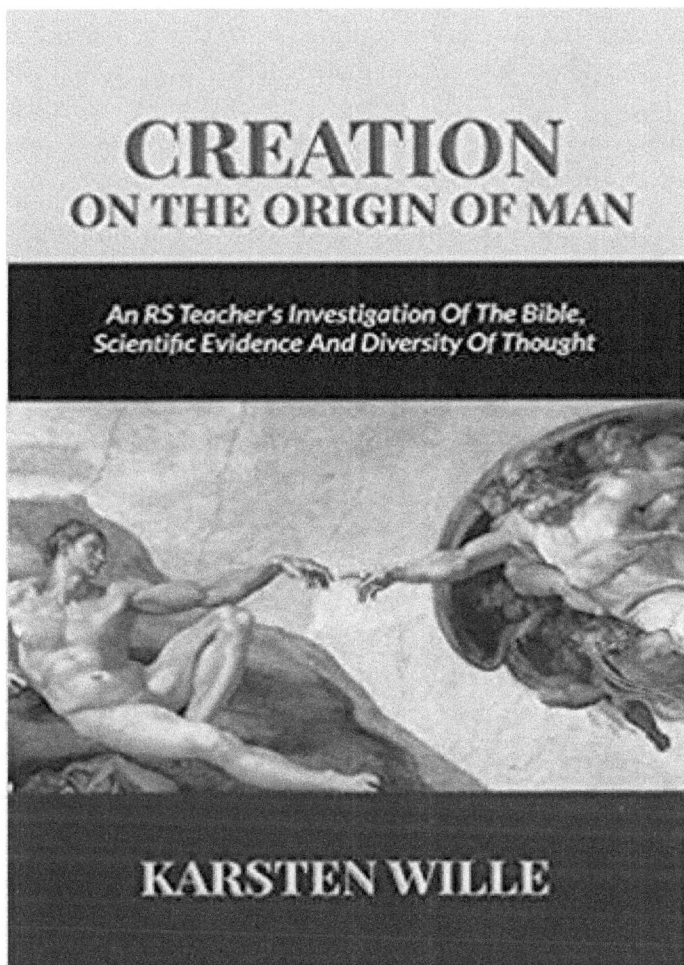

CREATION
ON THE ORIGIN OF MAN

An RS Teacher's Investigation Of The Bible, Scientific Evidence And Diversity Of Thought

KARSTEN WILLE

A Seasoned Theologian and Historian investigates all scripture, scientific sources and evidence based records on the origins of man.

There has never been a published scientific work that has shaped the world into a streamlined view, permeating the way we perceive the physical, biological and psychological sciences today such as Darwin's book 'On the Origin of Species'. His work has not just been confined to these fields, but has influenced both history and Christian Theology as well. The findings of Darwin have been readily accepted as a suitable explanation for the beginning of all life by the Catholic Church and other liturgical denominations.

This book seeks to question the validity of Darwin's 'On the Origin of Species', and whether it should be accepted by the Church as a suitable alternative to scripture. This will include the difficult task of discussing philosophy and science as a whole.

Karsten summarizes all the main points of the teachings of the church and scientific evidence.

ABOUT THE AUTHOR

Karsten is an international award winning author 'Tithing: Reviewing Scripture in context', and 'Creation: On the Origin of Man'. He has worked as a Pentecostal Pastor, planting churches in the UK and working in a Missions and Evangelism department ministering the Gospel in Africa, Asia and South America. With a PGCE from Exeter University and studies with the Open University in Educational Research, he has taught Religious Education mainly in Christianity and Judaism for the last 20 years. He also has a keen interest in apologetics.

Investigating the biggest questions in Christianity

www.ingramcontent.com/pod-product-compliance
Lightning Source LLC
Chambersburg PA
CBHW071802090426
42737CB00012B/1916